MARTIN LUTHER

TEXT BY PETER MANNS
PHOTOGRAPHS BY HELMUTH NILS LOOSE
INTRODUCTION BY JAROSLAV PELIKAN

Martin Luther

An Illustrated Biography

New Popular Edition

CROSSROAD · NEW YORK

1983
The Crossroad Publishing Company
575 Lexington Avenue, New York, N.Y. 10022

Originally published as "Martin Luther" © by Verlag Herder, Freiburg, West Germany
Translated by Michael Shaw
English translation copyright © 1982 by The Crossroad Publishing Company
This New Popular Edition copyright © 1983 by The Crossroad Publishing Company

Printed in West Germany

Library of Congress Cataloging in Publication Data

Manns, Peter.
Martin Luther: an illustrated biography.

Abridged version of book published in 1982 under the same title.
1. Luther, Martin, 1483—1546. 2. Reformation — Germany — Biography. I. Title.
BR325.M285132   1983   284.1'092'4 [B]   83-1783
ISBN 0-8245-0563-8

CONTENTS

INTRODUCTION

"Martin Luther the Reformer is one of the most extraordinary persons in history and has left a deeper impression of his presence in the modern world than any other except Columbus." So spoke "America's sage," Ralph Waldo Emerson, in a lecture on Luther delivered in Boston on February 15, 1835.

Luther was born in 1483; Columbus discovered America in 1492: that coincidence has long engaged the reflection, not only of American thinkers like Emerson, but of historians and of theologians, whether Roman Catholic or Protestant; and it may well serve as the occasion for some thoughts on the publication of *Martin Luther: An Illustrated Biography* by Peter Manns in America. For it is in many ways a continuation of that reflection on the coincidence of Luther and Columbus when the author of this volume, a Roman Catholic historian and theologian, finds it possible to speak about Luther's faith "from the inside" and sometimes even to identify himself with Luther's ideas and beliefs more closely than many Protestants (including, of course, Ralph Waldo Emerson) have been able to do. Perhaps the most impressive feature of the book for American readers will be the author's repeated emphasis on the continuities between Luther's pre-Reformation Catholicism and his stance as the Reformer; for we have been accustomed to concentrate on the discontinuities, as Luther himself tended to do when, in his polemical writings, he had to deal with challenges from the right or the left. The perspective of five centuries, the careful research of the last hundred years, and the far-reaching changes in the relations between Roman Catholics and Protestants—all of these factors make it possible for such a book as this to appear at all. For it to appear in America as well means that our life and culture, as well as our faith, may have special reason to attend to a portrait of Luther that has been drawn in this new way.

None of this would have been possible without the change of spirit symbolized by the Second Vatican Council. On one question after another, the Council manifested an attitude, as well as a method of theological thought, far more congenial to the Reformation than that of the First Vatican Council had been. To come from a study of Reformation debates about the doctrines of the Church, the ministry, and the sacraments to the decrees of the Second Vatican Council is a remarkable experience. Although the eventual outcome is, to be sure, a reaffirmation of traditional definitions of the priesthood, the seven sacraments, and papal authority, these definitions now stand in the context of a new and deeper recognition that the Church of Christ is in the first instance a body of believers, not an external institution, and that "priesthood" is a category that in the New Testament is applied either to Christ as High Priest or to all believers as kings and priests, but not to a special caste of the ordained. The arguments in support of such affirmations, moreover, have now become much more profoundly biblical, making use of the critical insights, historical research, and theological method that are characteristic of biblical theologians irrespective of confessional orientation. Conversely, it is no less remarkable an experience (as Dr. Manns shows) to come from the decrees of the Second Vatican Council to the debates of the Reformation. Many of the arguments employed by the adversaries of the Reformation—one thinks, for example, of the tortured reasoning in support of withholding the chalice from the laity in Holy Communion—cannot be defended, and no respectable theologian could get away with advancing them today.

Yet it would be an oversimplification to attribute this new picture of the Reformation principally to the "era of good feeling" represented and created by the Council. In many ways, the obverse is the case: the Council owed its reinterpretation of the Reformation, as well as its repossession of biblical theology, to the scholarly work of the two or three preceding generations, in which the distinctions between Roman Catholics and Protestants gradually became less significant for theological research. The work of several Roman Catholic historians—whose mentor was Joseph Lortz of the University of Mainz, where Peter Manns continues his work—raised up a new genre of Reformation research, which, building on the foundations of the medieval scholarship carried on by such giants as Martin Grabmann (1875—1949), sought to put Luther and the other Reformers into their late medieval setting and thus to understand both the strengths and the weaknesses of Luther in the light of the fourteenth and fifteenth centuries. These had been the very centuries that much of the "Thomist revival" had tended to denigrate in its zeal for "the thirteenth the greatest of centuries," with the result that the thinkers who came after Bonaventure and Thomas Aquinas—even the "Doctor Marianus" Duns Scotus, not to mention William of Ockham—did not receive the benefit of detailed scholarly research or even of critical editions. (The new edition of Duns Scotus, launched by the indefatigable Father Balić, still has a long way to go, while the Ockham edition, under the leadership of the Franciscan Institute at St. Bonaventure's, is moving toward completion, perhaps in time for the septicentennial of his birth in 1985.)

Out of such research has begun to come a new picture of the late Middle Ages, as well as a new picture of the Reformation. Many of the ideas for which Luther has been blamed by Roman Catholic polemics, or praised by Protestant hagiography, may now be seen as the common property of late medieval thought, shared (and often in a debased form) by his Roman Catholic opponents. One could say, therefore, that the scholarship of the twentieth century has begun to supply some of the missing quotation marks in the texts of the sixteenth century. The quotations to be identified are not, of course, only those from the late Middle Ages. The church fathers and even, *horribile dictu*, the Scriptures have not been credited as the sources for phrases and ideas that appear in Luther. It is, for example, a characteristic emphasis of Luther to regard the Virgin Birth, whose miraculous character he never doubted, as nevertheless a sign of the humility of Christ rather than of his sovereignty over the laws of nature; for, Luther said, Christ did not shrink even from being born of a Virgin. Protestant scholars, especially once they themselves had concluded that the idea of a miraculous Virgin Birth was an embarrassment, pointed to this as evidence for Luther's distinctiveness over against the patristic and medieval traditions. That distinctiveness, however, must be seen in the light of a sentence in the *Te Deum*, traditionally ascribed to Ambrose and Augustine on the occasion of Augustine's baptism and embedded in the canonical and liturgical life of medieval monasticism, especially of Luther's Augustinians: *"Tu ad liberandum suscepisti hominem non horruisti Virginis uterum,"* translated in the *Book of Common Prayer* as: "When thou tookest upon thee to deliver man, thou didst humble thyself to be born of a Virgin." It belonged to patristic and medieval piety, then, to see the Virgin Birth as part of the humiliation of Christ, and Luther continued to stand in this piety also after his separation from Rome.

The task of identifying Luther's sources is still far from completed, and in the course of editing the American Edition of *Luther's Works* there were repeated instances where it was necessary to supplement the meager apparatus of even the best critical editions of Luther by supplying the missing references. The standard set of Luther, the so-called Weimar Edition, was launched, with considerable fanfare, to mark the four-hundredth anniversary of his birth in 1883. As is the way of most scholarly editions, it has taken modern editors longer to produce the works than it ever took the original author. Unfortunately, the state of relations between Roman Catholic and Protestant scholarship—and, for that matter, the state of Roman Catholic scholarship on the Reformation—a decade or so after the First Vatican Council did not encourage the creation of ecumenical editorial teams for the planning and production of the Weimar Edition. (Even in the editing of patristic texts there was less ecumenical cooperation than the state of scholarship did warrant.) The quality of the Weimar volumes, uneven but still indispensable, would have been vastly improved if the critical apparatus had been able to benefit from the work of medievalists, especially Roman Catholic medievalists, as is evident from a comparison of the most recent volumes, some of them revisions of earlier Weimar versions, with the first volumes.

Still the Weimar Edition deserves a large part of the credit for the Luther renaissance of the twentieth century. Every generation since the Reformation had fashioned its own picture of the Reformer. He became, successively, an orthodox confessionalist, a Pietist, an Enlightenment rationalist, a German nationalist, a Romantic, a Kantian idealist, an existentialist—and, lest we forget, a Nazi and an ecumenist. But thanks to the availability of the texts of his early lectures in the Weimar Edition, and then to the discovery and publication of his long-lost lectures on Romans (found in the Vatican Library), scholars trained in the critical philological skills of the nineteenth century could set about disentangling the historical Reformer from these later pictures. Karl Holl (1866—1926) was such a philologist, whose work on the Berlin corpus of the Greek church fathers, beginning in 1894, was responsible for a splendid edition of an enormously complicated text, the works of Epiphanius on heresy (3 vols.; Berlin, 1915 — 1932). Bringing the same careful commitment to an examination of Luther's works, especially his early lectures, Holl produced a series of lectures and articles which, taken together (and published together), helped to turn Luther research in a new direction. His essay, "Luther's

Understanding of Religion," was delivered as a lecture in wartime Berlin on October 31, 1917, for the four-hundredth anniversary of the posting of Luther's ninety-five theses. It is still a monument in the interpretation of the Reformer, to which all of us who have worked in the field are profoundly indebted.

Nevertheless, the first section of Holl's essay, which deals with Luther's Catholic background, would have to be drastically revised today, as even a cursory comparison of it with the material in this book will show. It is a measure of how far we have come during the century since the first volume of the Weimar Edition that Peter Manns is in a position to refer to Luther not only as "the Reformer" (and that without the usual invidious "so-called") but as "father in the faith." In so doing, he has been able to set the record straight, over against earlier interpreters on both sides of the confessional boundary. His treatment of penance and indulgences is a good example, also because this was the issue in Luther's public emergence as Reformer. Professor Manns uses Luther's lifelong reliance on private confession (in which Luther differed from Calvin) as evidence that penance and confession were not, as such, the sort of legalism that Protestant interpreters have been fond of describing, but could be and sometimes were a genuinely evangelical force in the life of the Church and the life of the individual believer. On the other hand, Luther's failure to "find a gracious God" by means of penance and confession does not mark him as a pathological exception to the rule, as Roman Catholic interpreters have repeatedly charged, but rather as one who took the system at its word and then found that it simply did not work. With the author's similar treatment of monasticism, vis-à-vis both groups of Luther scholars, many readers, be they monastic or Protestant in their sympathies, may find it more difficult to agree. On the other hand, the work of Protestant historians, above all the pioneering researches of Heiko Augustinus Oberman of Harvard and then of Tübingen, is visible in the author's depiction of Luther's connections with post-Thomist scholasticism, especially nominalism.

Emerson's linking of the names of Luther and Columbus, with which this Introduction opened, suggests some additional considerations of special significance for an English-speaking audience. Despite the veritable cottage industry of Luther translations in Tudor England, well described by William Clebsch in his *England's Earliest Protestants* (New Haven, 1964), the mainstreams of Protestantism in England and America have not been dominated by Luther (or any other one man) as they have in Germany and Scandinavia. Consequently, the mythology of the Reformation in the Anglican, Puritan, Methodist, and Free Church traditions has acquired certain special features. It is, I think, more than a mere impression to note that English writers on the Reformation have tended to emphasize, more than their Continental colleagues have, the moral corruption of the Church against which the Reformation was directed, and proportionately to underemphasize the specifically doctrinal issues, on which so much of German theology has concentrated. Emerson's unease with Luther's dogmatism is an extreme instance, but it is not altogether atypical. Nor was the understanding of Luther made easier when his confessional descendants in America often tried to out-Luther Luther in their insistence on the purity of doctrine as a precondition for cooperation among Christians, even for prayer in common.

American Roman Catholics, for their part, brought with them from Catholic Europe many of the caricatures of Luther that had come out of the propaganda of the Counter-Reformation. It sometimes seemed that every candidate for the priesthood—and most catechumens—must have learned that Luther (a) said one should "sin boldly," (b) rejected the Epistle of James, and (c) married a nun; but meanwhile very few of them had so much as looked at, for example, the *Small Catechism* of 1529, whose "Evangelical-Catholic" exposition of the Apostles' Creed and the Our Father summarizes, without a wasted word, the consensus of the best in the tradition. Dependent as it has been on translations from French and German for so much of its scholarship, Roman Catholic theology in America has tended to lag behind the growing edge of that scholarship. Here, as in other chapters of intellectual history, it is instructive to ask what was translated and what was not, and why. To mention only one unfortunate instance, Jacques Maritain's *Three Reformers,* which even some of his disciples consider his worst book, found a translator into English, but Adolf Herte's *Das katholische Lutherbild* did not. In the past two or three decades, that situation is being ameliorated, thanks to the books of Roman Catholic scholars in the United States and Canada.

Martin Luther: An Illustrated Biography can serve as a corrective of the distortions of Luther and his Reformation that have marred the confessional literature in English. Above all, the Luther who emerges from these pages stands out as profoundly Catholic in his devotion to the

Church, to her creeds, and to her sacraments. Even when he denounced the Church for betraying the trust given to her by Christ, he was speaking in the name of that which the Church confessed and had taught him to confess. He was, if I may be forgiven for using the phrase again, an "obedient rebel." Neither Roman Catholics nor Protestants will find such a Luther easy to handle. Things were so much simpler when Protestant celebrations of Reformation Day in October 31 could be devoted to a litany about such evils as Mariolatry, celibacy, papal tyranny, and the practice of chaining the Bible; or when the pamphlets available in the tract of a Roman Catholic parish church could continue to portray Luther as a foulmouth, a psychopath, or even a suicide. These caricatures, which it is all too easy to caricature in turn, have now yielded on both sides to the more complex but also more accurate picture that becomes visible in the paintings and photographs as well as in the text of this book and that will, I dare say, be visible no less in the many other books on Luther being published in this anniversary year.

Can the man who is usually blamed or credited for tearing us apart help to bring us together? That may be too much to hope, at least for the present. But the cause can only be aided by a book about this man that dares to tell the truth. For, as an authority acknowledged both by Martin Luther and by his adversaries declared, "We cannot do anything against the truth, but only for the truth." It is a pleasure to welcome this beautiful collection of pictures and this provocative collection of historical information as a major contribution in English to our common quest for that Truth.

Jaroslav Pelikan
Sterling Professor of History
Yale University

By 1516 Martin Luther had already developed from his family's coat of arms the sign of the Luther Rose, which he explained as a symbol of his theology. In a letter he says: "The first should be a cross: black at the heart [center], its natural color, that I may remind myself that faith in him who was crucified makes us blissful. For the just man will live by faith, faith in the crucified. But such a heart should be in the middle of a white rose, to show that faith gives joy, comfort, and peace; therefore the rose should be white and not red, because the color white is the color of the spirits and all angels. Such a rose stands in a field the color of heaven, to show that such joy in the spirit and in faith is the beginning of future heavenly joy. And in such a sky-blue field a golden ring, to show that such bliss in heaven lasts forever and has no end and is also precious beyond all joys and possessions, just as gold is the highest, noblest, and most precious metal."

I

1. THE GENERAL HISTORICAL SITUATION

To provide a relatively accurate characterization of Luther's age as it affected his development and activity is a task as difficult as it is challenging. Even the ordinary observer and reader should, at the very outset, be made aware of the limits to which such an attempt is subject.

All history, but especially the history of the age to be considered here, is mysterious in its inner workings, and while such mystery can be made visible, it cannot be made wholly transparent. The question as to the significance the historical situation may have for the distinctiveness, development, and activity of Martin Luther as a concrete individual is even more difficult to answer. For Martin Luther is more than the sum of historically discoverable influences. He is no bottle whose content can be determined by analyzing the ingredients.

With that warning in mind, what precisely is the relevance of the historical situation if we interpret it objectively and carefully?

We begin with Emperor Maximilian I (1493—1519), who reigned over the "Holy Roman Empire of the German Nation." His epithet, "the last knight," gives a fair indication of his significance: the knights had been replaced by mercenaries and foot soldiers; their splendid armor no longer afforded protection against the fire-spewing muskets, mortars, and drakes. Military service had stopped being a matter of knightly honor and loyalty, for the emperor now had to pay if he wanted to feel that he could rely on the faithfulness of his mercenaries. Any number of "new things" were being invented and discovered, or made their appearance in the hearts and minds of men. The new had not yet burst the old, magnificent frame but it was becoming clear that it could not be accommodated, that cracks were running through the structure, and that men reacted to them both in joy and in fear.

The imperial question came to affect Luther's biography directly when Maximilian died and the pope, in league with France, first promoted the candidacy of the French king Francis I and then that of the imperial administrator, the Saxon elector Frederick the Wise, in order to thwart the election of the candidate of the imperial party, the excessively powerful Charles V. For a brief moment, the political situation was more favorable to Luther and the Reformation than at any other time in his life. Out of consideration for the elector, the heresy proceedings against him were dropped. And because Frederick the Wise could not be bought off with money, the secret papal diplomacy dangled the Golden Rose before him, and the cardinalate before one of his friends, a friend who could only be Luther. A cardinal's or a heretic's hat, such was the momentary alternative in this tense situation, at least from the perspective of the papacy.

Yet the real crisis of the papacy during this time was more encompassing and deeper. Ushered in by the "Babylonian exile" of the popes in Avignon, it continued in the "Great Schism" where first two and then even three popes excommunicated each other and sucked Christianity dry. It reached the height of mortal danger under popes like Sixtus IV, Innocence VIII, Alexander VI, Julius II, and Leo X. While all of these popes became patrons of the artists of the Renaissance and bibliophilic collectors of precious manuscripts and books and thus recovered the cultural leadership of Europe, and while their wars and alliances took the political and financial power of the papal state to previously unattained heights, it was precisely through these activities that the popes unfortunately compromised for a long time to come their real task, the leadership of Church and Christianity.

In an anonymous lampoon entitled *Julius exclusus,* the great Erasmus alludes to his benefactor, the martial Julius II, and skewers a typical representative of this papacy with his pointed pen, exposing him to mockery and public contempt. Even Luther repeatedly rejected this malicious pamphlet for its causticity and destructiveness. Yet just a short time later, he became convinced that the representatives of this overbearing papacy had to be seen as agents of the Antichrist within the Church, and combatted as such. Without wishing to excuse Luther's radical antipapal polemics which soon became unbearably rude, one will have to concede that it was enormously difficult and perhaps impossible for him to acknowledge the popes of his time as successors of St. Peter and representatives of a universal pastoral office. If anywhere, it is in the papacy of the period that we have the principal cause of a central malfunctioning which necessarily affected the entire life of the Church.

What was true of popes, the College of Cardinals, and

the Curia applied proportionately to the bishops and their aristocratic cathedral chapters, as could be documented instructively by the example of the cardinal archbishop of Mainz, Albrecht of Brandenburg. In spite of his rumored love for a baker's girl, he was no incarnation of moral degeneracy but a prince of the Church who, after a passing indecisiveness, courageously resisted the Reformation and remained loyal to the old Church. But he was also wholly a child of his time who saw no problem in uniting in his person no less than three episcopal sees and the electorship, and who had no scruples about paying off his pressing debts in Rome by that trade in indulgences that was to usher in the Reformation. What excuses him in a human sense is at the same time what is truly scandalous here: the unperceptive matter-of-factness with which he, like so many of his peers, did what was visibly wrong.

Where Luther was born, in Kursachsen, one of the smaller German territorial states which was developing well under the government of Frederick the Wise (1486 – 1515), conditions were incomparably better. We have already mentioned the incorruptibility of the elector who was modest and intelligent enough to reject the imperial dignity that was offered him after Maximilian's death, an act that earned him not only the appreciation of the princes but of the entire German people. The epithet "the Wise" had originally been conferred on him for his knowledge of courtly etiquette. But he soon earned it also for his intelligent restraint in government and his developed sense of justice. If one adds his great kind heart and his modesty, Frederick emerges as one of the most appealing personalities among the princes of the period. Being a man of considerable piety, he was a passionate collector of relics which, partly with Luther's help, he bought up everywhere. In the castle church at Wittenberg which he built himself, he then installed and exhibited them to the credulous as objects that would bring about the remission of sins.

The elector, who had humanistic interests, had, in 1502, founded a university in god-forsaken Wittenberg because he had wanted to annoy his cousin, Duke George of Saxony; and that institution was to become very important for Luther's development. But the intelligent protection which his prince afforded him in all his troubles was to prove even more important for the future reformer. A kind of mystery shrouds the relationship between the elector and the young monk and professor. For Luther never came to know his prince personally, presumably because the elector believed that it was only on this condition that he could protect him effectively. Even Wittenberg was not free of signs of profound tension.

On the eve of the Reformation, profound dissension marked the entire spiritual and intellectual situation of Christianity. Though there were occasional compromises and syncretic forms, the theology of the universities and of the studies carried on in the religious orders was dominated by the confrontation of the more or less irreconcilable approaches of the *via antiqua* and the Occamistic *via moderna*. The old opposition between conciliarist and papalist theology heightened the tension. The new approaches of the "Platonic Academy" or of what was otherwise the quite encouraging reforms of a theology that went back to the Bible and the Church Fathers merely created confusion. There were signs of a danger that communication between the various styles of thought and systems might cease.

Pre-reformist and late-medieval popular piety in its wide-ranging forms is even more confusing. Although there was certainly no lack of primitive superstition, dangerous superficiality, and crude exploitation of the sacred, it would be falsifying reality were one to deny the profundity and genuineness that could be found, in the personal sphere, in the striving for inwardness and spirituality, and in the sphere of communal piety, in sermons and church music, but principally in religious art. Yet when we examine the inner connections more closely, two insights suggest themselves immediately: the overall impression confirms what was said above about the inner conflict as a consequence of a pivotal malfunctioning of life. The entire situation also suggests that the old Church was incapable of assimilating the abundance of positive approaches; as a result, it was principally in connection with the Reformation that they became effective and productive.

A complete analysis of the historical situation would have to deal with the development of a new human image and a new life-feeling, the simmering unrest that first seized peasants, visionaries, and apocalyptics and then spread to the entire social structure and transformed it. Whenever Luther's biography calls for such a more thoroughgoing treatment, we will return to these matters. For the moment and in conclusion, it will suffice to note that the Reformation had become historically inevitable (J. Lortz). In terms of the image of a profound organic malfunction of the life of the Church, this means that the Church of the popes, which naturally did not stop being a church, went to great length to cure the symptoms of an illness that kept it from credibly and effectively fulfilling its mission in Christendom. Unfortunately even Luther did not succeed in immediately bringing the necessary cure. True, the intensity of his concern provides the thrust toward that depth in which an effective cure had to begin. But the unavoidable defense and the equally unavoidable onesidedness of the attack unfortunately led to a life-threatening shock that caused the unity of Christ's Church temporarily to disintegrate although this had not been Luther's intent. It was a condition that was not rectified until the Church succeeded in a common effort to institute a comprehensive reform in whose course the concerns of the Reformation were brought to fruition.

2. LUTHER'S BIRTH, HIS YOUTH AND SCHOOLING, HIS ALLEGED "FATHER COMPLEX"

After the preceding reflections on the historical background, we now report as simply as possible on Luther's life, beginning with his birth, his parents, and his schooling.

Martin Luther was not a native of Eisleben although the accidents of his life brought it about that he died between two and three o'clock in the morning of February 18, 1546, in the very same town in which, according to Melanchthon, he was born into this sad world shortly before midnight on November 10, 1483. The date of birth is less certain than the date of death, however, for neither Luther nor his mother were completely sure about the former. We only know that it was shortly before Martin's birth that the parents had come from the region around Eisenach and that by early summer of the following year, the family moved to Mansfeld, a fact which can only be explained by the father's profession. The house in which the child was born still stands. Judging by the impression it makes, the family can hardly have belonged to the poorest of the poor. We know nothing precise about the age or marriage of the parents. There are two conflicting versions concerning the mother's Christian and maiden names. According to one, the mother, whose Christian name sometimes appears as Margaretha, sometimes as Hannah, was a Ziegler and thus the daughter of one of the wealthiest peasant families in the village of Möhra, the place of birth of both parents, which lay some three hours' walk south of Eisenach. According to the second version,

which I take to be the more reliable one, the mother was a Lindemann and came from a respected burgher family in Eisenach.

There is no doubt, however, that Hans Luder, Martin's father—a name that may be derived from Lothar—came from an old landowning family in Möhra that has continued to inhabit its village of origin and its hereditary position as small landowners into the twentieth century. Since the High Middle Ages, they had been free landowners who only paid a small ground rent and whose only master was the elector. They were well-to-do and debt free without being actually wealthy. The precondition for the preservation of their property was a law of inheritance that made it possible to avoid all division of property. It was always only the youngest son who inherited, a circumstance that naturally had unpleasant consequences for the older siblings if marriage into another landowning family proved impossible. This had happened to Martin's father, "Big Hans," as he was called, who, being the eldest of four sons, had no right to the inheritance and therefore saw himself obliged to take up the mining of copper schist which was carried on in neighboring Kupfersuhl.

Although Big Hans was thus no farmer but a miner, Luther maintained throughout his life that he was a farmer's son and of peasant stock. Nevertheless, beginning with his school days, Luther actually developed as a person who had been molded by an urban culture, and he invokes his peasant origin to underline the progress from peasant son to professor and adversary of the pope. Yet he would have obtained the same effect had he emphasized with equal vigor his origin as the son of a "poor miner." We will see in a moment that, oddly enough, Luther did not do this, or did it only infrequently, and not with the same insistence. For compared with that of a farmer, his father's profession was difficult, interesting, and quite modern. In other words, due to his father's profession, little Martin grows up in a nearly modern ambiance yet makes nothing of that fact.

In both a technical and an economic sense, the profession of miner made demands on the father that were not easily met. The copper schist, which in those days was either strip-mined in the Mansfeld area or mined at a shallow depth, was smelted on charcoal and worked into crude copper. Such foundries were either hereditary property or rented from the counts of the region. Luther's father was such a lessee. Quite apart from the technical effort, the running of a foundry not only required luck in the finding and sale of the ore but some knowledge of economics and considerable capital to pay the wages, construct the mines, and keep the furnaces going.

After extremely difficult beginnings, Big Hans did not escape any of the worries and risks that attended such an enterprise. It seems that he had some initial success, for he soon made his appearance as one of the "Four" who represented the community vis-à-vis the council in Mansfeld. But he had to work hard and count every penny. In 1505, there were still four sons and an equal number of daughters to provide for. By 1510, he seems to have made it. Three daughters and Martin's younger brother Jacob, who had taken up his father's profession, married into mining families. The plans his father had for Martin can also be understood from this perspective: smelters always found themselves embroiled in some legal dispute and constantly needed cash, and this is the reason it was expected that little Martin would come to the aid of the firm in the quickest possible way through the study of law and a wealthy marriage. But "man proposes and God disposes," and unfortunately He does not always dispose as man proposed. This applies to Big Hans not only with reference to his son.

It is obvious that the extremely difficult years during which the father, beset by constant financial worries, tried to build a life for himself and his family through hard work did not fail to have some effect on Martin's childhood. Whenever Luther speaks of that childhood and his parental home, he remembers poverty, thrift, and severity. He does not forget that his overburdened mother had to gather the necessary firewood in the forest and carry it home on her back. And he remembers all his life that his study cost his father "much sweat and hard work."

As in families the world over, it was the severe, angry father, a man who always lived under stress, that set the atmosphere in the home. The stories the older and rather loquacious Luther tells about these matters in his *Table Talk* are sufficiently known. Being late and much emended recollections, they require careful interpretation and should not be read like the diary entries of a child or the records of a center for the prevention of child abuse. There is, in particular, the story according to which the irate mother thrashed the poor boy until she drew blood for having stolen a nut. Luther goes on to comment—and this has stimulated interpreters of all persuasions—that it was this severe upbringing that drove him into the monastery, an explanation that is anything but reliable, however plausible it may sound. In another report about the "stolen nut," Luther says of his father that he "whipped

Title page of *On the Freedom of a Christian Man* (November 1520), which, with its prefatory letter to Pope Leo X, represents the last attempt at reconciliation and was inspired by Karl von Miltitz. This is the last of the three great programmatic works of 1520.

me so that I ran away and felt ugly toward him." But Luther also mentions that after this severe punishment his father did everything he could "to win me back." This suggests that Big Hans was no inhuman tyrant but simply an excitable father with principles who apparently could not always restrain himself. Like many sons who remember a strict father, Luther then goes on to say that the beatings did him no harm.

In addition to the murky reports in the *Table Talk* which are difficult to interpret, there is other documentation and especially facts that cast a somewhat kinder light on the grim picture of the thrashing parents. There are, first, the two houses in Eisleben and Mansfeld in which Luther spent his childhood. If one allows the impression these two buildings make to sink in a little, one will concede that Luther was one of those fortunate beings who never lacked a "home." This home saw more than work, punishment, and upbraiding; it was also a place where people sang, celebrated, and even played. Since the road leading from the house in Mansfeld to school occasionally turned into mud and filth, the child was carried to school when this became necessary. We are thus entitled to feel that little Martin was given a very human and Christian education albeit not an individualized one. The world of the spirit, which made such a deep impression on Martin in his childhood, even stood up under the learned and often polemical criticism of the reformer, as is impressively proved by Luther's unbroken love for the Mother of God, the Guardian Angels, and the beloved saints.

Because the father, a man who had never seen the inside of a school, was concerned about this, little Martin was given a sound education. It is probable that the father began sending the little fellow to the Mansfeld town school on the feast of St. Gregory, 1488, which he attended for eight years until he had learned everything it had to offer. In the spring of 1497, his father sent him, along with Hans Reinecke, the son of one of his father's business associates, to the cathedral school at Magdeburg, run by the Brethren of the Common Life. The next year Martin was moved to another school in Eisenach, where he spent the last three years of his schooling with relatives.

Luther's *Table Talk* leaves us with a terrible impression of his incompetent teachers and their almost devilishly refined punishments. What is called for, however, is a thoroughly critical examination which has its point of departure in the fact that the fear little Martin felt of school and family must be see as the norm and that we must resist the temptation to represent Luther's childhood and school days in the light of later reports or to see them from the perspective of our modern sensitivity and view them as a "martyrdom." An abundance of important facts supports such a decision: when all is said and done, there can be no doubt that Luther learned a great deal in that reviled school, such as Latin, for example, and most assuredly not the dog Latin of Scholasticism nor just the crude combination of Latin and German which, as the *Table Talk* and the sermons show, he mastered with great perfection. The Latin he learned served as the foundation of all knowl-edge and was a thoroughly alive, creatively used language.

All in all, we would raise the following objections to the primitive or "scientifically" stylized legend of Luther's martyrdom at home and in school: Having completed the first stage of schooling, Luther left his parents' home in Mansfeld when he was fourteen years old and thus at an age when most of the famous children of the Middle Ages had long since finished their *trivium*. Philip Melanchthon was just twelve when he went to Heidelberg University. From that perspective, our Martin rather strikes one as a "late bloomer" who had trouble leaving the family nest.

Like a sponge, Martin absorbed all the impressions the "big city" of Magdeburg, with its population of twenty-five thousand, had to offer. An even stronger shaping force seems to have been the impressions in Eisenach, in the home of his relative Konrad Hutter, the sacristan of the church of St. Nikolas, or in the home of the mayor, Heinrich Schalbe, at Kunz Cotta's, or in the merry circle around the Franciscan friar Johannes Braun. It seems that it was among Braun's friends that Martin first consciously experienced the veneration for St. Anne that was soon to give a decisive turn to his life. In Eisenach, he was also impressed by the happy marriage of the Schalbes and came into contact with remarkable women such as the mayor's wife and her daughter Ursula Cotta who were so utterly different from his overworked mother back home.

The development of young Martin, which took an apparently seamless course without deep external or internal crises and whose result for that very reason is very suggestive, becomes apparent here. Already in Eisenach, the distinctive quality of the young scholar's entire background was clearly "no longer peasantlike but urban, that of a burgher" (M. Brecht). If it is equally true that throughout his life Luther invoked his peasant origins and simply ignored what strikes one as the modern ambiance of a smelter's family in which he spent his entire childhood, we can infer something of importance here which gives us a clue to his entire development. For if his father's professional world and the plans for the son that came out of that world were alien and always remained so, the decision he made a few years later to become a monk does not represent a break in his development but was germinally present all along though not in the form of a conscious motivation. But for that very reason, the distance he felt toward his father's plans and the development this gave rise to must never at any moment be interpreted as a conscious or unconscious "protest" against the father.

3. STUDY IN ERFURT: FROM BACHELOR OF ARTS TO MASTER OF ARTS

With the summer term of 1501, the beginning of his studies at Erfurt University, an important new phase began for Martin. Much could be written about this town with its twenty thousand inhabitants and prestigious university which had been founded as the fifth German university after Prague, Vienna, Heidelberg, and Cologne. But more important than any number of scholarly details is the observation that none of the ideas and expectations young men today connect with their move from school to university can be applied to Luther's time. For while it is true that the eighteen-year-old escaped the caning of the schoolmasters by this step, he did not exchange the compulsion of school for the academic freedom which even the merest beginners at our universities invoke these days. Rather, medieval universities were institutions that in their teaching tended to tighten rather than to loosen the close ties that bound students to the school. This is something the young man who registered as "Martinus ludher ex Mansfeld" discovered when the dean of humanities asked which college he had chosen. For it was by compelling the student to live in one that the university effectively supervised the life style of its charges. In Erfurt, the refusal of a college to accept a student was tantamount to exclusion from the university.

We do not know with complete certainty which college Luther chose. According to a number of sources, he decided in favor of the smaller, well-reputed St. George's, which was close to the Augustinian friary and which the students jokingly called the "Beer-Bag." According to other sources, it was the famous Amplonian college near St. Michael's Church, popularly known as "Heaven's Gate," in which Luther took up residence. But whether "Beer-Bag" or "Heaven's Gate," the residential rules and education were the same. From "wake-up" call at four in the morning to "lights out" at eight in the evening, the daily schedule was minutely ordered. The students slept in large dormitories and studied in halls set aside for the purpose. Two meals were served at ten in the morning and at five in the afternoon, with meat being served four times a week. The food was substantial and adequate. Exercises began at six in the morning and were followed by lectures that were resumed after the morning meal and continued until five o'clock. During the study period, the students were not allowed to leave the building and the closing time of the gates was strictly enforced. Although beer was served in the college, gambling, excessive drinking, and relations with the opposite sex were banned. The students had to speak Latin with each other, wore a uniform, and were expected to participate in daily mass and the canonical hours. In sum, it was a schedule and an order that could not deny its monastic model. Instruction and study at the humanities faculty were similarly regimented.

As early as the end of September 1502, Luther was admitted to the bachelor's examination which he passed elegantly rather than brilliantly or, to put it differently, with average grades. He now had to wear the dress of the baccalaureus and, although still a student, he also had to assume certain teaching duties in grammar, rhetoric, and logic.

In January 1505, he concluded his philosophical study with the master's examination. This time, he passed brilliantly, that is, as the second in his class. As a sign of his new dignity, he was given the master's reddish brown beret and ring. His inaugural lecture was followed by the customary ceremonies consisting of a feast and a torchlight parade. Luther, who loved such festivities, incurred considerable expense, and the proud father, who henceforth stopped addressing his son with the familiar second person singular, never balked at paying for it all.

This is the place to consider briefly the significance the study of philosophy had in Luther's later development. This applies particularly to his way of thinking and his learning and teaching methods. Throughout his life, Erfurt exerted an influence on Luther's analysis of texts, the organization of his ideas, the formulation of his theses, conclusions, and proofs, his type of controversy, and his delivery. His passionate fight against Scholasticism notwithstanding, Luther always clung to the form and method of the Scholastic disputation, that is, he considered it suitable to ground, give greater depth to, and defend the truth that he drew from the Bible and the theology of the Fathers. The way of thinking that goes along with disputation cannot be radically separated from the underlying logic, the laws of thought, and the concept of truth that characterize the Scholastic philosophy he had learned in Erfurt. This means that even as Luther developed into an "antiphilosopher," he always remained the "philosopher" in a certain sense, and "philosopher" was also his nickname at college. Ultimately, it is this "academic" schooling and style of thinking whose absence he repeatedly rather arrogantly criticized in his controversy with the Swiss reformer Zwingli who, being an autodidact, had not had such an education.

1 House of the Luther family in Mansfeld where the family moved from Eisleben in 1484.

2 Hans Luther († 1530), Martin Luther's father. Painting by Lucas Cranach the Elder (around 1527).— Wartburg Collection.

3 Margarete Luther († 1531), Martin Luther's mother. Painting by Lucas Cranach the Elder (around 1527).—Wartburg Collection.

4 References to the Wartburg as the seat of the landgraves of Thüringia occur as early as 1080. Around 1200, the castle was enlarged by Landgrave Hermann I and restored in the nineteenth century. From 1498 to 1501, Luther attended school in Eisenach and later lived disguised as "Junker Jörg" in the Wartburg in 1521/22 where he translated the New Testament into German.

16

ANNO · 1 5 30 · AM · 29 · TAG · IVNIJ · IST · HANS · LVT
D · MARTINVS ·   · VATER · INN · GOT
ERSCHIE   DENN ·

IIO · 1531 · AM · 30 · TAG · IVNY · IST · MA

ETA LVTERIND · MA   RTINVS · MVTTE

NN · GOTT ·   ✦ VERSCHIEDE

5   View of the cathedral (14th cent.) and the church of St. Severus (13th—15th centuries) in Erfurt. Luther began studying in the faculty of arts of Erfurt University in 1501. He was ordained in the cathedral in 1507.

6   St. Anne carrying her daughter Mary with the child Jesus on her arm. Statue (around 1330) on the "Triangle Portal" of Erfurt cathedral. Luther knew this statue of St. Anne whose help he implored when he almost died in a thunderstorm near the village of Stotternheim on July 5, 1505, and vowed to become a monk.

7   Cloister in the Augustinian monastery in Erfurt which Luther entered as a novice on July 16, 1505.

8   Luther as friar. Colored woodcut by Cranach the Elder. Luther is wearing the cap of a doctor of theology which he became in 1512.—Bretten, Melanchthon Museum.

Because there are inconsistencies, it is not easy to say how significantly the nominalism of Erfurt influenced Luther's intellectual and spiritual development. But we can sense more or less which elements may have had a positive, and which a negative, impact. Nominalist logic, though not epistemology, clearly proved stimulating, and nominalist theology with its emphasis on faith and Scripture and its rejection of reason in this sphere could not fail to make an impression on him. But from the very beginning, Luther also rejected the hollow abstraction of nominalist thinking as he did the theology of the schools that resulted from it and that was alien to the Bible. He did not care for bloodless abstractions and insisted on the priority of "substance" over "grammar" throughout his life.

To the extent that it was already stirring in Erfurt at the time, humanism also affected Luther. It testifies to Luther's intellectual flexibility that the worn path of a prescribed academic order did not keep him from making use of the elective humanistic offerings.

Having passed his master's examination brilliantly, Luther had to give lectures and hold exercises in the faculty of humanities. But he also could and was supposed to begin study at one of the higher faculties. How, and for which faculty, would he decide?

4. THE ATTEMPT TO STUDY LAW, STOTTERNHEIM, THE MONASTERY

The career the proud father took for granted was something the son was aware of and had never rejected, but it was certainly not a carefully considered and settled matter. Since medicine and theology were out of the question, the law remained as the only alternative that, except for reservations Luther himself did not clearly understand, had everything on its side.

So he returned to the university where he had to begin giving his lectures as a master of arts on April 24 and where, seemingly as a matter of course, he began his new studies on May 19, after the solemn faculty mass in honor of St. Ivos of Chartres, the patron of the Erfurt jurists. There would have been no problem if Luther had not broken off his newly started studies a few weeks later and made a decision no one was prepared for. What had happened? What reasons for Luther's behavior can be found?

Anyone with some knowledge of human nature and some familiarity with the reactions of talented young scholars will first ask whether there might not be reasons that are related to Luther's feelings about the law. Even students of his caliber feel at first that there is much that is interesting, yet drop the discipline after some initial familiarity because they recognize instinctively that it will never make them happy. This supposition receives some support from the fact that Luther later not only continued to express his distaste for the law, because he considered it uncertain and dependent on interpretation and subject to distortion, but specifically mentioned, in the course of one comment of this sort, his youthful reading of the commentary of the great jurist Accursius.

There are other clues which may be interpreted as signs of an inner process which, in its entirety, will probably remain Luther's secret. There are sources, for example, that report a curious melancholy at this time which the sudden death from the plague of two fellow students who had passed their examinations with him explains only in part. But the thought of death and anxiety over one's salvation prompted many young men to enter the monastery in those days.

This is what the scant sources tell us about Luther's state of mind when, on June 20, right in the middle of the semester, he abruptly left Erfurt to visit his parents in Mansfeld. He never indicated the reason for this journey. His father may have called him home to discuss his marriage, and the possibility that he was simply tired of the law cannot be excluded. All that is certain is that the monastery was not discussed by either father or son. Luther merely reports that he made the long journey to Mansfeld on foot which took three days at least. This is also how he had traveled home during the Easter vacation of the preceding year. On that occasion, his sword had become entangled between his legs and had torn a vein in one of them, causing a life-threatening wound because the loss of blood had been severe. With his swollen leg in a tourniquet that soon came loose, he had had to lie down and wait for a physician. Facing death, he had implored the Mother of God for help but had made no vow. Although his recovery at home did not proceed without complications, he soon dismissed the danger from his mind and, while still abed and recuperating, learned to play the lute without benefit of a teacher. On the return journey from Mansfeld to Erfurt on July 2, 1505, Luther reacted in a significantly different way in an almost identical situation. A few hours' walk from Erfurt, near the village of Stotternheim, a violent thunderstorm overtook him. Lightning struck close to him and hurled him to the ground. In mortal fear, he called on St. Anne for help and added the vow: "Help, St. Anne! I will become a monk."

This vow had a marked effect on Luther's relatives and friends and also on wider circles of the Erfurt public although reactions differed. Later, it was through Luther himself and the indignant reply of his enemies that it became the slogan in the fight for and against monasticism. To this day, it is quoted again and again by biographers, historians, and theologians, and not infrequently it is misunderstood. But those scholars who deserve to be taken seriously are unanimous in their belief that Luther's vow, however sudden, represents the result of an inner development which the sources at least hint at.

As always in such cases, there were friends who understood and supported his decision. But others felt the world had collapsed and went to great length to get him to change his mind. It can be neither asserted nor denied with absolute certainty that there was also a weeping young girl among these latter since no halfway dependable source mentions anything of the sort.

Most people, though not nearly all, were convinced that a supernatural power had intervened in Luther's life: his angry and powerless father thought it must be the devil and the work of witches. Johann Nathin, Luther's teacher in the monastery, on the other hand, compared the Stotternheim episode to the conversion of St. Paul before the gates of Damascus.

It says something for Luther's realism that he never used that comparison, although at a later time he never hesitated to identify with Paul. Luther reacted as both a Christian and a human being. He did not simply rush from Stotternheim into the monastery but took two weeks to consider the consequences of his decision, to say his final good-byes, and to burn his bridges behind him. If, in retrospect, he mentions "remorse" during these weeks, it is a recollection which, like many others relating to his monastic life, portrays reality inaccurately. What is true about the recollection is that he felt the heavy burden the fulfillment of his vow meant for him.

Thirty-four years later, he will remember that memorable day: on the eve of the feast of St. Alexius, the evening of July 15 (not July 16 as biographers erroneously date it), Luther called his friends and acquaintances together for a last meal before they escort him to the monastery on the following day. His friends cried when they embraced Martin a final time at the gate of the "Black Cloister," as it was popularly known. But Martin persevered and, his later bitter criticism of monasticism notwithstanding, went through with a decision which, as an act of total surrender to God, he never disavowed. Thus he states in his *Table Talk* of July 16, 1539, that God has understood and accepted his Stotternheim vow and his invocation of St. Anne "hebraically": "Anne" means "through grace" (Anne or Hannah is related to the Hebrew word *hēn* meaning "grace" or "favor"), "not according to the law" (in the sense of the merely legally enforced fulfillment of a promise). All in all, even the entrance into the monastery manifested divine grace and a divine promise. This is the reason there is no absence of light in this difficult hour, and that light will continue to shine, especially in the Black Cloister.

II

1. THE ERFURT CLOISTER: FROM NOVICE TO FRIAR AND PRIEST

As the gate fell shut and his dejected friends were left behind, another gate opened onto a kind of life that was certainly not altogether new to Luther but only reveals itself for what it truly is to the person who commits himself to it without reservation.

It is part of the experience of all religious orders that the decision to embark on such a life requires thorough scrutiny, both by the applicant and by the order and the superiors. Luther began his life as a religious with the so-called postulancy which lasted for about two months. In addition to conversation, the general confession he made to the prior was an important element in his examination by the superiors. Advising the parents, whose consent did not constitute an indispensable precondition for admission according to church law, was part of a clarification the prior considered important. Luther therefore wrote them from the monastery. Big Hans raged with anger and disappointment. He renounced his son and went back to addressing him with the familiar, and in this case reproachful, *du*, as he had before the master's examination. The death of two sons and the rumor that Martin also had died as well as the mediation of relatives gradually induced the father to bow to the inevitable.

A few comments on the history of the Erfurt monastery are in order. Established in 1266, it became the largest monastery in both the Saxon Province of conventuals and in the Reformed Congregation. In the early fourteenth century, Erfurt became the seat of the order's own course of general studies *(studium generale)*. Because the Augustinians furnished the city with a professor of theology in order to save tax money, a tie between the order and the university was established. Famous teachers, such as Heinrich Friemar the elder, Jordan von Sachsen, Johann Zachariae (who had allegedly defeated Hus in a debate at Constance and lay buried before the altar), or Johann Bauer von Dorsten and his disciple Johann von Paltz, had been superintendents of studies.

In the Erfurt cloister, Luther was to see and experience all those things for which he later so bitterly reproached monks and Church. Here, it is important to understand that this was undoubtedly a source of the most dangerous abuses but that the reform-minded Erfurt Augustinians initially avoided them or kept them within tolerable limits.

It is also in this context that one should judge the comment that the constitutions of the Augustinian Hermits did not regulate the life of the friars in accordance with the vow of poverty, or did so insufficiently. This is the reason why, during times of decay, there were Augustinians who, like the monks and canons of the older orders, owned property and money, a circumstance which could not but contribute to the decay of the entire communal life of the friars. In the Erfurt observant cloister, such massive degenerative symptoms were absent, of course, but we know from observations Luther made that the friars did own small amounts of money that allowed them to defray certain everyday expenses. Yet when one scrutinizes these statements—such as Luther's recurring complaint about his old, worn cowl which his own means did not suffice to replace—one finds that they do not really testify against, but to, the concrete and real poverty of the Augustinians of the period.

We have now reached the point where we can report his life as novice and friar in the Erfurt cloister primarily from Luther's recollections. This does not mean, of course, that we can rely completely or even principally on Luther's late statements. The only method we can adopt is to take these retrospects into account but also to make use of reliable sources to correct those misrepresentations that occur for a variety of reasons when someone looks back on his life.

For the sake of greater clarity, I begin with a list of the most important dates: if the postulancy lasted for only a few weeks or two months at most, then Luther's novitiate began sometime during the fall of 1505. Since we know the length of the probationary period, it is at the earliest in the late summer of 1506 that Luther can have been admitted to profession and thus to the order. There followed the minor and the major orders whose dates we do not know with absolute certainty: the subdeaconate on September 19 or December 19, 1506; the deaconate on February 27, 1507; and priesthood on April 3 of the same year. Ordination in all cases was by the suffragan Johann Bonemilch who resided in Erfurt and was the titular bishop of Laasphe. From these sparse, reasonably certain dates, a number of important conclusions can be inferred:

It was the Erfurt superiors, not Staupitz the vicar general, who destined the highly talented Brother Martin—a man called by heaven itself, it seemed—for the career which reached its first culmination in the taking of holy orders. In view of the education of the ordinand, the superiors considered a scholarly preparation unnecessary, that is, they felt that a purely "technical" preparation according to Gabriel Biel's exposition of the mass was sufficient. The study of theology began directly after ordination. This seems to suggest that from the very beginning, the superiors never destined Luther for pastoral duties but for an academic career. With a view to his further development, they hastened the course of things to such an extent that they had to make use of their power of dispensation since on April 3, 1507, Luther was not yet twenty-five, the canonically prescribed age for ordination.

This overview and our conclusions suggest that we need not consider further the question of Luther's theological career and can concentrate all the more intently on his spiritual preparation for the religious life and priesthood, a matter that was of eminent significance for his development as a reformer. Following the daily schedule to which Luther had to submit since the beginning of his novitiate at the latest, we begin with external and physical matters. The Divine Office orders the life of the Augustinian as it does the schedule of all monks. Late at night, between one and two in the morning, the bell rouses the sleeping friars for Matins. At dawn, the actual morning prayer of the friars, Lauds, is sung. Subsequently, the community proceeds in carefully ordered rank to the chapter in the chapter house. Prime follows at six after which the community celebrates mass. Terce at nine is the beginning of the so-called Little Hours with Sext following at noon and None and Vespers at around three in the afternoon. After dusk, the day ends with Compline.

The first impression a layman has as he considers this schedule is that the friars never left the church. But this impression is misleading, as we shall see in a moment.

We begin with the simple matter of sleep which appears to have been much too brief. If we remember that even the medieval monks lived according to solar time and in principle without artificial illumination, we quickly realize that about eight hours sleep during the night in wintertime and about six during the summer plus one hour of rest in the early afternoon before None add up to a number that certainly did not affect health adversely. The friars slept in a white wool tunic in their unheated cells,

which was bearable considering that they were hardened. Nor was their physical hygiene dictated by the ascesis of the desert Fathers. They washed daily, using water they themselves blessed upon rising. They shaved head and beard at regular intervals and even bathed on certain days of the year. Their linen underpants and white socks were washed, regularly, of course.

Meals followed a similar pattern. Except for periods of fasting, the friars had their noon meal shortly after twelve, the evening meal around six. Like all Christians, the Augustinians abstained from meat on Fridays and on the vigils of great saints. During the periods of fasting—from All Saints' Day till Christmas and from the Sunday before Ash Wednesday to Holy Saturday—Wednesdays and Saturdays were days of abstinence. In addition, the evening meal was reduced to the consumption of some beer and wine and side dishes such as gingerbread or fruit and salad. The prior could order an appropriate diet for the sick or those young friars who required it.

As we move from externals to what lies below the surface, we briefly mention the monastic "rubrics." In liturgical texts, *rubrum* refers to the rules in red (Latin *ruber*) ink or print that lay down what prayers are to be chosen and specify all the ceremonies down to the lighting and extinguishing of candles. Like the liturgy, the entire life of the monk—from rising in the morning until bedtime, from his conduct during choir office and the numerous and different reverences, from behavior at table, during study, and on journeys to the sign language during the *silentium* and extending to the bell signals and the order of dress—is governed in the most minute detail by precise rules whose violation is punished by a variety of sanctions. Learning all of these rules took up a significant part of the novice's time. The danger to dependent personalities from such an excessive ordering of all aspects of life is obvious. But it is equally obvious that in a world of matter and spirit the inner requires the outer, and this applies not just to intersubjective relationships but also to man's life with God.

Similar considerations apply to the choir office in which the inner and spiritual act of the praise and adoration of God is embodied in the *opus Dei* of the praying community: the "work of God" consisting in psalms, hymns, lessons, antiphons, responses and versicles, and prayers. The choir office is the original form of monastic prayer, and at a very early date it became the model for all prayer in church. It may even be said that the history of the choir office or of the breviary provides us with a clear indication of the greatness and wretchedness of the pilgrim Church. We should add that all of the criticism Luther later expressed had already been expressed before him, that the rebukes were certainly not unfounded and, at the very least, did in fact point to serious problems, yet that a onesidedly negative criticism simply does not do justice either to the nature of the choir office or to the Erfurt practice of it. For a critical examination of this entire set of questions, three key terms which we encounter time and again in the history of the choir office and its reforms suggest themselves:

The term *quantum* has to do with the length and extent of the breviary. The Augustinians, who as mendicant friars were not really monks in the sense of the old monastic orders, used the Roman breviary, like the Franciscans, rather than the considerably longer monastic one. According to this breviary, the nightly Matins lasted a little more than one hour. Even though Lauds was directly followed by chapter, the friars had time until Prime at six which they could spend in contemplative prayer, the reading of the Bible, study, or the celebration of private masses. The intervals between the Little Hours, which lasted hardly more than fifteen minutes, were even longer. Things were arranged in such fashion that the public choir office ended and climaxed in the personal, meditative prayer of the individual friar. But the choir office undoubtedly also had the considerable advantage that, if only quantitatively, it consisted largely of psalms and Bible readings which, due to the choral singing and the nature of the reading, especially impressed themselves on the memory. If Luther, like countless medieval monks before him, later knew the Psalter and extensive passages of the Bible by heart, this was due less to personal study than to the much maligned choir office.

Of course, the choir office also had its dangers and problems. This can be demonstrated easily by the silent prayers that were said in preparation for the choir office. For here, the Lord's Prayer or the recitation of the creed became simply a way of measuring the duration of a silence that should actually have served the meditative preparation for the choir office. A quantitatively determined quota of prayers always brings with it the danger that those who pray will not understand what they pray, or will understand it only in part. Luther's criticism of the medieval choir service, especially at the cathedral chapters, is undoubtedly not without justification. But such criticisms are not fundamental and do not, or cannot be shown to, apply to the choir office at Erfurt.

The choir office, or the Hours, must then be considered from the point of view of the *officium,* that is, from the point of view of the service that every monk must perform. The one who prayed or sang what did not correspond to the set order, who ignored the set times, or omitted parts of the breviary became guilty of a venial sin. But he who failed to pray the Hours altogether was considered a schismatic because he had refused the service that was owed to God. Anyone who has ever taken seriously the obligation to participate in choir office or the breviary knows what this means. It is not the obligation as such that is problematic. For the person who means to lead a spiritual life, be it as monk or as priest, simply cannot do so without regular and intensive prayer. But this obligation does become problematic when it is given a petty and anxious or a legalistic interpretation.

In the end, one will have to ask whether the picture of a Luther whom monasticism has turned into someone who is excessively scrupulous and who gradually frees himself from this nightmare by reading the Bible really corresponds to what happened. If it could be shown that this is not the case, then stories of this sort are all part of a "Luther legend" and either the product of the editors of the *Table Talk* or Luther's own doing. In looking back on his life, he may have succumbed to the temptation to use the stylistic means of hagiography to embellish his past "for the greater honor of the pure Gospel."

The final key term to be used in a critical evaluation of the choir office is the phrase *opus Dei* ("work of God"). It is true, of course, that the breviary and, more particularly, the solemn choir office involved a good deal of training and effort. To the extent that Gregorian chant or what was taken for it had not been drummed into them in school, the novices had a great deal to learn. There were, in addition, the previously mentioned red rubrics that were much more difficult to memorize than the rules of conduct which finally became routine. Part of this drudgery is learning how to read and pronounce correctly, to learn how to comprehend and vocalize the biblical and other Latin texts in a dignified manner.

Apart from the rubrics, Brother Martin did not have the slightest technical difficulties. There are, of course, other matters that might be mentioned and which underline that aspect of the choir office that is mere drudgery. It is only natural that the office should become no more than a routine performance when simple monks succumb to the temptation to place the "quantity" of completed psalms into the scale before God or when they anticipate their eternal reward for the trouble of the psalmody in this life and insist on being honored above all others *pro psalmis et lacrymis* ("for psalms and tears"). The service also becomes drudgery when it tortures and tyrannizes the conscience as a falsely understood obligation or, conversely, when it degenerates into a kind of ascetic high-performance sport.

I will not dispute that such degeneration has occurred in history, or that it might recur at any time for as long as men succumb to the temptation to look for nothing but their own advantage in whatever they do. What I do dispute—and this in part by invoking the "reforming" Luther—is the secret imputation that the choir office is such drudgery by its very nature. Should that be true, I wonder who, in Erfurt, might have encouraged and seduced the novice or friar to engage in such an effort. It cannot have been the wise old novice master nor the fatherly prior who most likely coined the comment about the hotheads among the young friars who always wanted to knock down twelve pins even though a mere nine were standing in the lane.

Luther did have difficulties with the highly structured and regimented common prayer. He preferred the personal, free-flowing *oratio mentalis* ("mental prayer"). The constant constraint which interfered with or even suppressed his unusual spontaneity was even more disturbing to him in reciting the office in private than in public. In the course of time, however, Luther found solutions for his problems, and they were not that he simply stopped praying. One needs only to compare the praying friar and the praying reformer, for such a comparison readily shows that prayer as the "work of faith," the structure of the community's liturgy, the length of public or private prayer, the kneeling and crossing oneself, the binding order of prayer in church and family, or the biblical substance of prayer were none of them things that disturbed the reformer at all. But the comparison also shows that the vilified choir office with its psalms, hymns, and sequences left a resounding echo in the songs and liturgical texts of the reformer. However, it is certain that what the praying Luther allegedly lacked so completely, the "certainty of the heart" and the "confident Amen," may never be taken as matters of course, nor can they be readily obtained through the choir office.

Of considerably less significance for the spiritual life of the friars was the chapter of faults which, during Luther's time in the monastery, took place only once a week. There is no question that the monks made a clear distinction between guilt to be acknowledged in chapter and sin to be confessed privately. The sources also leave no doubt that Luther was not driven into any sort of guilt complex, however seriously Brother Martin may have taken his monastic obligations.

With sin, we come to sacramental confession, and with confession to all those real or putative torments Luther suffered in this connection if the customary accounts are to be credited. And due to the idea untold people have of confession, these accounts are taken as fact. Without prejudice, we will first attempt to clarify what place confession occupied in the life of the monks, and what confessional practice was like.

From its beginning, monasticism had an instinctive discernment of sin in its many forms and its mysterious power over the heart of man. The constitution of the Augustinians made it the friars' duty to seriously examine their conscience every day, and to confess once a week. The regular confessor was normally the prior, and it was he alone who could forgive mortal sins such as serious sexual transgressions or theft. Venial sins could be confessed to any friar-priest. To the extent that confession served spiritual guidance, the friars turned to specific father confessors such as the novice master or other experienced fathers. In addition to weekly confession, there was the general confession which comprised the entire life or certain extended periods of it. It was obligatory only at the time of admission to the monastery. At other times, it was used with circumspection, and care was taken to avoid repetitions unless there was a clear need. As in the case of all Christians, confession consisted of as complete and contrite an avowal of sins as possible by the penitent, and the absolution and imposition of an appropriate penance by the confessor. In addition to guides for the examination of conscience, there were manuals like the *Summa Angelica* by Angelo de Clavasio which Luther knew and did not esteem highly.

But what concrete knowledge of Luther's practice and of his father confessors do we actually have?

According to his later recollections, Luther made much more frequent use of confession than the rule prescribed so that the sources initially convey an impression of morbid scrupulosity. For Luther not only confessed thoroughly but claims to have done so for hours. He clearly doubted the validity of his confessions and for that reason questioned the efficacy of absolution. Not content with a general confession to the prior, he says that there were two additional ones: one in Erfurt to the *praeceptor*, by

9   Slab covering the grave of Johann Zachariae, one of the principal accusers of Jan Hus at the Council of Constance, in front of the high altar of the Augustinian church in Erfurt (13th cent.). During his profession and reception into the order in the early summer of 1506, Luther prostrated himself on this slab.

10   In Rome, Luther stayed in the monastery of the Augustinian Hermits, next door to Santa Maria del Popolo.

11   View from the tower of the castle church in Wittenberg of the façade of the town church. After his return from Rome, Luther was sub-prior of the Augustinian cloister, preacher, and professor of biblical studies here.

12   Johann Tetzel, O.P. (ca. 1465—1519) was a preacher of indulgences on behalf of Pope Leo X, who needed money for the construction of St. Peter's in Rome, and Cardinal Albrecht of Mainz, who could not repay his "pious debts." The banking house of Fugger had lent this prince of the Church a large amount of money which was to be repaid in this fashion. The traffic in indulgences was the occasion for Luther's theses in 1517.—The woodcut shows Tetzel preaching with a chest of money and a letter of indulgence; above is the bull of indulgences and Pope Leo X, whose bull on the rebuilding of St. Peter's gave rise to the indulgence dispute.—Constance, Rosgartenmuseum.

LEO DECIMVS

BULLÆ INDUL

IOHANNES TETZELIUS, LIPSIENSIS
MISNICVS MONACHVS ORDINIS SANCTI DOMIN

1520

13   Tower of the castle and the castle church at Wittenberg which also became the university church in 1503. In this church, which was renovated in 1885/92 in neo-gothic style, Luther's solemn promotion took place on October 19, 1512. It is uncertain whether he affixed his ninety-five theses which were intended as a call to a disputation to the portal that served as the university "bulletin board." Luther still lies buried in this church.

14   Martin Luther, colored woodcut by Lucas Cranach the Elder (circa 1520).

15   Dr. Johann Eck (1486—1543), professor of theology at Ingolstadt University, was Martin Luther's adversary in the Leipzig disputation during the summer of 1519. —Detail of the bronze epitaph of J. Eck in the church of Unsere Liebe Frau in Ingolstadt.

16   Devils are leading a pope and a bishop into the jaws of hell. This relief in wood which was created in Franconia in the early sixteenth century clearly shows the disappointment and the anger people of the period felt toward the Church of Rome and its head. It is such feelings that led to Martin Luther's Reformation. —Collection in Coburg Castle.

which term he may have referred to the novice master; the second one later, in Rome, where the powers of the father confessors were especially extensive and certain. There are comments that testify to Luther's anxiety concerning the completeness of his confessions: he claims to have run back to the priest when, having just finished, another sin occurred to him. Later, as a priest, he reports that, having already confessed in preparation for mass, he signalled to the father confessor at the altar and confessed a second time while it was in process. According to his recollections, monks cannot get enough of confession: "We wear out the father confessors," he writes.

If we had to credit these and similar statements, we would have to judge that Luther was a pathological case whom even the art of modern psychotherapy could never have cured completely.

But the comments that have come down to us are not persuasive and can be questioned under a variety of aspects. They are not the diary entries of a tormented and self-tormenting monk but the *Table Talk* of a reformer who is wholly sure of himself and who, addressing his friends, colleagues and disciples, points to the tortures of a dark, long-since mastered past. In statements in which Luther does not cite his personal but the common experiences in accusation of the malpractice of monastic confession, this becomes especially evident. But since even in his recollections Luther does not denigrate the past as a matter of principle and since he makes quite positive statements about his former father confessors in this context, we find a good many irreconcilable elements and even contradictions in the reports.

If we judge the Erfurt practice of confession by looking at Luther's father confessors, it becomes impossible to sustain the thesis that seeks to account for Luther's crises over confession by postulating a growing rebellion against the fundamentally wrong system of Catholic confession as practiced in the monastery. But a thesis which is usually put forward by Catholics and according to which Luther really was the pathological case that is mirrored in the retrospects can be refuted even more easily. For is it likely that his confessors who were also his superiors would have admitted a neurotic, a person of notorious scrupulosity, to the novitiate, profession, and ordination, and later to the teaching of theology and leading functions in the order? It is very important to develop a clear picture about all these mistaken judgments that so clearly stem from denominational prejudice. For only then do we get closer to a reality that is much more complicated than his-

torians and especially theologians are prepared to admit even today.

But what more deeply relevant questions can be raised here, once it has been shown that Luther was no psychopath and the sacrament of penance no fundamentally un-Christian horror? Are Luther's difficulties with confession, like his difficulties with the choir office and the chapter of faults, no more than minor complications, the result of a few improper exaggerations and differences in personal style? That even as a reformer Luther clung to regular and frequent private confession throughout his life, indeed that he considered it a source of strength and consolation without which he could not have resisted the temptation of the devil, would seem to point in this direction. But such an indication does not take us very far. It is only the question why something that tormented and frightened him in the monastery should later have strengthened and consoled him that will open up new perspectives and backgrounds. The fact of the matter is that there is a whole number of texts in which Luther keeps repeating that he remained uncertain of the absolution granted him after confession, or that he doubted that God had truly forgiven his sins.

On the other hand are statements that do explain Luther's doubts about forgiveness, are plausible, do not require a far-fetched interpretation, and take his actual situation into account. I am referring to the not so very rare passages in which he mentions that he did not always succeed in mobilizing the required contrition. In back of this lies a large problem that has to do with the theology of penance but that plagued Luther not as a theological but as a practical problem. We are dealing here with the concrete question whether in confession "attrition" is a sufficient disposition for the forgiveness of sins or whether a contrite heart is indispensable. Anyone who reflects a little about this because he feels the burden in his own heart will soon understand something he didn't understand before. For if someone feels attrition, it is because he fears purgatory and hell and does not wish to lose the promised bliss of heaven. He thus thinks first of himself and only secondarily of God because he fears and needs Him. But the person who feels contrition feels deep in his heart how much his sins conflict with the love of God, the love He feels for us and the love we owe to Him. Everyone who has ever been touched by that true and great love is familiar with the shame that is connected with attrition. And he or she knows with an equally intimate knowledge the difficulty or even impossibility of a repentence in which we wholly disregard ourselves out of love for God or where we finally love ourselves for God's sake alone.

This suggests Luther's dilemma which inevitably developed into the crisis whose spiritual and theological solution determined his whole life and work. At this moment we are concerned only with the first tentative steps on a long path. Still, it must be said even at this point that this path proves how great the heart of the young friar was and that it is a path we take because we are led, not because we choose it on our own.

Back to Luther and the questions that beset him at the time. With the instinct of someone who is being guided, he rejected attrition as a solution and did not look for reassuring counsel in the conventional piety of the day. Instead, he stayed with the demanded contrition which was unattainable to him, and thus involved himself in a maze of irresolvable questions. The harder he tried, the more clearly he realized that the will has no power over the love of the heart. The less he felt the remorse of such love in his heart, the more uncertain became the remission of his sins. It was a perfect circle. How did Luther escape from it?

From this perspective, a number of otherwise incomprehensible statements make sense. For what does it mean that Luther doubts his own purity and believes all remaining impurity to be ineradicable? The moment we interpret impurity as the impure desires of a love directed toward the self, the remark becomes perfectly clear. On this basis, Luther's difficulty in distinguishing between venial and grievous sins can be explained with equal ease. Both involve the incapacity to love God with the love that is owed Him, both separate from God.

These considerations also suggest why all the excellent advice of eminent father confessors could not help Luther and why even Johann von Staupitz could not resolve the matter. For in his situation, what good could the advice to put all hope in God's mercy do him? Or what use was the reprimand: "God is not angry with you, you are angry with God?" The young monk therefore found himself alone with his problem. But we must remember that at that time Luther saw neither the full depth nor scope of the problem and that theoretical helplessness does not necessarily exclude various kinds of practical remedies. The problem Luther had to deal with from this moment on did not lead to an unbearable permanent burden, let alone a rapidly accelerating crisis which he then solved by a single stroke as hell was staring him in the face. If such a primitive comparison is admissible, Luther experienced something like a toothache. The pain set in suddenly or faded, a condition that did not preclude times of euphoria. The pain returns as long as man has teeth, and as long as he reaches out in hope and faith to perfect his imperfect, pathetic love.

It is obvious that the problem we have sketched had a central bearing on the few remaining points still to be discussed. This applies especially to Luther's attitude toward life in the monastery for which he prepared for an entire year during his novitiate and to which, acting as a free agent, he totally committed himself by a vow in the fall of 1506.

It will be shown that despite his rejection of a corrupted monasticism, Luther never disputed the meaning and justification of a binding monastic vow. Luther's fundamental question reemerges here, for he is concerned with a vow that commits us to a loving, and therefore free, surrender to God and neighbor. Once again, the problem lies in the connection of freely given love and a wholly serious lifelong obligation.

His later recollections with their massive criticism of the busywork of the Erfurt Augustinians strike one as ideologically exaggerated and simply do not correspond to reality. There is absolutely no basis for the charge of arbitrarily chosen, conspicuous works (*opera electitia et speciosa*) of rigorous asceticism in the areas of fasting, penitential exercises, and inhuman obedience by which monks allegedly distinguished themselves from ordinary Christians and gave themselves airs as a privileged class. Quite the opposite is the case. In its reasonable strictness, the "roughness" of the life of the Augustinian friars rather makes a blessedly normal impression. Everything is oriented toward the service which the friars have to perform in the ministry, at the university, or in schools. From prayer and intensive study in preparation for teaching and preaching to a poor but certainly not exaggeratedly poor life, it is difficult to discover any "work" that Luther did not also do as a reformer. After his profession and during the years thereafter, he behaved as if he would never leave the monastery. His colleagues and superiors seem to have thought so, too, for already in 1508 he ranked in sixth place among the dignitaries of his convent.

In conclusion, Luther's training for the priesthood, his first mass, and his devotion to the mass must be dealt with at this point.

As suggested above, Luther's preparation for ordination was primarily practical and did not include the study of theology, a procedure that was not at all unusual at the time. Since the celebration of mass represents the most important priestly function, preparation centered on this task. Luther used the standard work of the Tübingen theologian and nominalist Gabriel Biel, the *Canon Missae,* which first appeared in 1499. Reminiscing about his studies, he recalls that his heart had bled while he read it. Here, we once again encounter Luther's fundamental problem which became significantly more acute as he considered the solemn celebration of the mass and the reception of the physically present Christ who was also understood to preside over the final judgment.

What made him dubious about the remission of sins in confession made him all the more skeptical about the worthiness of which an upright Christian had to be morally certain before he received the Eucharist. Luther already had difficulties with the daily communal mass at which the friars were to communicate at least sixteen times a year. In both intensity and scope, these difficulties increased considerably after Luther had been ordained and had to take on the task of holding private celebrations of endowed masses at the monastery. In addition to the mere participation in the Eucharist, it now was necessary to celebrate mass correctly.

According to his reminiscences, Luther's first mass on May 2, 1507, turned into an occasion where all these difficulties combined and almost precipitated a crisis-like collapse during the Canon, when he claims to have succumbed to the overwhelming majesty of God whom he must address, directly and without a mediator, in order to offer Him, the living and eternal God, the gifts of the altar. According to his reminiscences, Luther wanted to rush away from the altar and would supposedly have done so had the assisting priest, the prior or the novice master, not restrained him. Although it is difficult to interpret the various versions of the report, the historicity of the reminiscence is not in dispute.

Although I have no desire to question the historical core of the recollection, I consider this retrospect, like so many others, to be seriously flawed. Nor does the incident become more credible when one remembers that such stories about first masses were told more than once during the Middle Ages. Seen properly and reduced to its presumably true core, Luther's reaction was a quasi-normal difficulty which many conscientious neophytes experienced during their first mass, and continue to experience today, a fact which finds nearly official confirmation in the liturgical office of the *presbyter assistens.*

From this perspective, Luther's fear during his first mass and his later masses must be defined as serious moral distress but has nothing whatever to do with a pathologically onesided temperament. The horror story of a Luther still "confessing" during mass should be relegated to the same realm of "Protestant legend" as the "Catholic story" which Cochläus reports according to which the young monk once collapsed with the cry, "It is not I," when the biblical story about the cure of the deaf-mute was read during mass.

More credible in this connection are those reminiscences that testify to Luther's high regard for the office of priest during the celebration of the mass and which also mention his occasional euphoria when he had succeeded in celebrating mass in the way expected of him. It may also be that he succeeded in combining his devotion to mass with the veneration of the saints. But it is not here that we should look for the core which brought Luther in the course of a rather long development to view the mass as a real horror. What is meant here is the mass as "sacrifice," applied to the needs of the living and the dead; in short, the mass that was being exploited for personal advantage and misused as magic, the so-called "corner masses" of countless mass priests and monks who lived off the business they did with the Most Holy. But years were to pass before this kind of mass became a problem and an insupportable scandal for Luther. Compared to his fellow friars and later fellow reformers, Luther here appears as an archconservative who only laboriously detached himself from the traditional form of the mass, the silently prayed Canon, the Latin text, and the priest's vestments, and who continued to adhere to the old view in his understanding of the physical presence under the forms of bread and wine and in his idea of the administration and reception of the Eucharist. If one refrains from polemical formulas and relates the later criticism to false forms of the theology and practice of the mass, it becomes anything but easy to distinguish between Luther's lifelong high regard for the Eucharist and the purified Catholic mass.

We therefore conclude our reflections on this important point by observing that the neophyte's problems with the mass were nothing out of the ordinary though it is true that they were the cause of weighty concerns. It should be added, however, that neither these difficulties nor the anxiety-creating question concerning the love of God intensified to the point where they became a fundamental crisis that would unambiguously account for our young priest-monk's subsequent development.

2. FROM STUDENT OF THEOLOGY IN ERFURT TO PROFESSOR IN WITTENBERG

Although Luther's future seemed settled, it appears that there were monks and superiors in the Erfurt monastery who tried to hamper the dramatic rise of a friar who was allegedly being compared to St. Paul. For example, Father Martin was assigned to the cleaning of latrines and begging in the countryside — a story that has a marked flavor of monastic legend about it. But even if Luther should really have come into contact with cleaning rags and beggar's sack, this cannot have gone on for long, for we know that directly after celebrating his first mass and as early as the summer semester of 1507, he immediately began the study of theology. In the interest of saving space, I will confine myself to indicating the technical details of the curriculum. In Erfurt, Luther would first have had to attend lectures, especially on Peter Lombard, for a period of five years, and would also have had to go through the prescribed disputations. But he earned his doctorate in five and one-half years because the statutes provided for shorter courses for monks, courses which could be shortened even further when necessary or when a student enjoyed special favor.

Luther benefited first from the interest Johann Nathin, professor of theology and head of the *studium generale*, took in him as long as he made his own the views of his teacher on policies to be pursued by the order. Since Nathin belonged to the circle of Erfurt nominalists, Luther had probably come to know him during his philosophical studies. As a teacher of theology, Nathin did not make a deep impression on him although his marginal comments on Peter Lombard's *Sentences* and on Augustine betray the influence of the Occamist tradition which prevailed in Erfurt. Luther still believed that man's will is free and that, at least indirectly, he can by his good works earn the merit that God then rewards through His grace. It is not His absolute power and arbitrariness but His compassion that is emphasized. To the extent that man does what he can, God will not withhold grace. More important are the beginnings of a critique of Aristotle and of an Aristotelian theology. Luther recognized ever more clearly that we must orient our thinking by the Bible and that the "rancid rules" of logic do not suffice to measure God in His revelation.

It should be added that in keeping with the custom of the period Luther had also been a lecturer in philosophy in the Erfurt *Studium* since the summer semester of 1508.

His studies were considerably speeded up when, in the fall of the same year, the vicar general, Johann von Staupitz, called him to Wittenberg as lecturer in philosophy because his predecessor, Wolfgang Ostermayr, had been given a leave. Here Luther spent a rather joyless year lecturing on Aristotle's *Nichomachean Ethics*. But that he could now pursue his theological studies under the direction of Staupitz, who was the dean of the theological faculty at the time, was a considerable benefit. For obvious reasons, Staupitz now hastened his student along. On March 9, 1509, Luther qualified for the *baccalaureus biblicus* which was followed in the fall of the same year by the examination for the *baccalaureus sententiarius*. Even before the newly graduated baccalaureus could give the public inaugural lecture which was customary after this examination, he was transferred back to Erfurt, perhaps because he was urgently needed, perhaps because his superiors did not wish to see him working in another monastery and at another university.

But since Luther's order politics, which had been the same as those of Father Nathin, changed after his return from Rome, as he now adopted the views of Vicar General Staupitz, considerable tension developed between Luther and the extremely sensitive Nathin. To resolve the complicated situation, Staupitz ordered Luther's transfer to Wittenberg, and in September 1511 he and Johann Lang returned there to stay. The Erfurt people did not immediately understand what this loss meant, and when they finally did, it was too late. For the chapter of the Reformed Congregation had taken the following decision in May 1512: Lang was to take over the teaching position in philosophy that Luther had occupied a short time earlier as a substitute and which, along with the Bible professorship, was part of the teaching obligations the Augustinians had assumed at the new university. Luther was made sub-prior of the small Wittenberg friary in which, after his promotion, he was to assume the direction of the *studium generale*. Behind all this, one senses the machinations of Staupitz who gave up his professorship in 1512 and therefore needed a successor because his obligations in the order began to take up more and more of his time.

In view of this background, it makes no sense to allege that after his arrival in Wittenberg, Luther's situation was wholly indeterminate. For it is precisely the famous scene under the pear tree in the cloister yard that proves that as regards the plans of the order everything about Luther's future had in fact been settled, and this in spite of the fact that after the promotion of 1511 Staupitz could have chosen among any of a number of candidates within the order. But in sending Luther on for the doctorate in theology and in commissioning him to preach to the community, the vicar general and his councilors had decided that he should finally be given the position to which his talents predestined him. That Luther, having thus had his future laid out for him, immediately listed fifteen reasons why this should not be done and claimed that, for reasons of health, he was simply unable to bear up under the stress of the tasks assigned to him can easily be explained by the humility of the friar or the literary cliché of the late reminiscences and must not be interpreted as proof of Luther's indecisiveness, let alone rejection of the plans that had been made for him. The same applies to Luther's letters on this subject in which he states that he is not interested in obtaining the doctorate in theology and that he had resisted the plans of the vicar general to the point of disobedience and reemphasizes his incapacity and his unworthiness for such a task.

Quite apart from Luther's inner difficulties, there were also personal reasons. The Wittenberg teaching post with its numerous compulsory lectures and disputations, the simultaneous course of studies and new examinations in 1509, the unusual hardship of the journey to Rome, the new theological lectures, and the quarrel over matters affecting the order had all taken their toll. If one remembers in addition that Luther never in his life changed positions with flying colors, it becomes perfectly understandable why, in his new situation, Luther should have preferred obedience to impulsive decisions of his own. The greater the temporal distance from the event and the more insight into the significance of his change in course grew, the more urgent became the need to make the entire later development with its unforeseeable consequences a matter of the obedience of faith, not the result of personal decision.

From the perspective of the historian, it was probably perfectly simple and ordinary reasons that caused the delay in Luther's promotion and the assumption of his teaching post. Among them was the simple fact, for example, that neither Staupitz nor the monastery had the money to pay for Luther's promotion fees because such a large number of Augustinian theologians had obtained higher degrees in 1511, which is why Staupitz had to persuade the elector to assume this burden. With the assurance that the biblical professorship Staupitz had given up would be taken over by Luther for life, Frederick the Wise finally paid. On October 12, 1512, Staupitz received the required fifty gulden from the court treasury in Leipzig.

In October 1512, Luther finally received the doctorate, the preparatory acts of candidacy, permission of the chancellor, and the oath of obedience to the Church having been attended to. The ceremony took place on the morning of October 19 in the castle church. With admission to the senate of the theological faculty on October 21 and a final defense, Luther had now become a full-fledged professor.

Even today, the important question concerning the date and nature of Luther's first Wittenberg lecture cannot be answered with absolute certainty. We do know, however, that in the winter semester 1513/14 he lectured on the Psalms and that these lectures, the so-called *Dictata super Psalterium* continued on into the winter term 1514/15, and perhaps even to the following summer semester. But it is quite possible that another set of lectures preceded this one, and that his subject may have been the Epistle to Titus or Judges or perhaps Genesis, especially the story of Abraham which Luther treated throughout his life in sermons and lectures. It is certain that he lectured on the epistles of Paul—Romans (1515/16) and Galatians (1516/17)—and the Epistle to the Hebrews (1517/18) in the following years. In the winter semester 1518/19, he turned back to the Psalms. He gave two-hour lectures, at six in the morning during the summer, at seven during the winter. Beginning in 1516, he lectured at one in the afternoon.

This unusually crowded schedule was supplemented by a number of disputations and countless sermons which he gave in the monastery or the town church. Apart from further marginal comments and the quickly swelling correspondence, there were publications on the Seven Penitential Psalms or sermons on the Ten Commandments and the Lord's Prayer.

If Luther really did hesitate to accept the task that had been chosen for him, then our esteem for Staupitz grows, for on the basis of objective criteria this man ignored all the subjective doubts of his disciple and was confirmed in his judgment. As professor of Bible, Luther proved himself. Using the Bible as his guide and working his way through all the distortions of Scholastic theology, he found his way back to the beginnings of biblical theology in which the story of Abraham or of Christ happens anew for every reader, as it were. This is the reason why neither the ecclesiastical condemnation of certain exaggerated pronouncements nor a systematizing inclusion in a supposedly "reformist doctrine" which cannot be derived from

Luther's work allows us to quickly dismiss it. Luther also proved himself as a preacher. For the theology that concerned him not only demanded that he proclaim it, it is ultimately identical with such proclamation. That is why the most profound direction of his teaching cannot be understood without his preaching.

3. LUTHER AS FRIAR AND SUPERIOR OF HIS ORDER

As we search for relevant sources and facts, we remember, first of all, Luther's unbroken and successful monastic career. As early as 1508, Luther is part of the elite of the Erfurt friary. This is shown not only by his position as lecturer but by his previously mentioned journey to Rome on business of his order in the winter of 1510—1511.

That the order placed great confidence in Luther is further indicated by the fact that in 1512 he was appointed sub-prior of the Wittenberg cloister and, on May 1, 1515, vicar provincial of the ten Augustinian houses in Meissen and Thuringia for a period of three years. If as sub-prior he was the second ranking superior of the Wittenberg cloister, he now had the spiritual and canonical responsibility for ten important communities such as Dresden, Erfurt, Neustadt, Orla, Gotha, Langensalza, Eisleben, Nordhausen, and Magdeburg whenever the vicar general was absent, which was often.

As vicar provincial, Luther had to fulfill the entire range of obligations of a superior, if we can judge by the correspondence that has come down to us. They extended from participation in financial dealings to the canonically prescribed visits to monasteries under his jurisdiction between April and June 1516, and included the support and guidance of a prior in difficulties, the demotion of that official and the election of a suitable successor, the counseling of the new Erfurt prior, Johann Lang, in delicate questions of monastic order such as the complicated issue of flight from one monastery and the joining of another, the counseling of other superiors, and the rendering of spiritual help to difficult and troubled monks. It would be an attractive task to set forth the picture of Luther as vicar provincial, using his own letters and biographical documents as a basis. I confine myself to roughly sketching the upshot of such a portrayal. In the mirror of this three-year correspondence, Luther emerges as a model friar and superior of the monasteries and friars under his jurisdiction. He is thoroughly familiar with the rules, the constitutions, and the general law of the order. As superior, he

Title page of Luther's first celebrated reforming work of 1520: *To the Christian Nobility of the German Nation concerning the Reform of the Christian Estate.*

distinguishes himself by his psychological knowledge, his judgment, and his friendliness, but equally by the courage to make authoritative decisions. All in all, he is wholly and without reservation a friar, a Christian, and yet already the Luther we know, even though still wearing the cowl as if it were part of his body.

Of greatest importance in this connection are letters such as the one dated April 5, 1516, which he sent to his former fellow monk Georg Spenlein who had been transferred to Memmingen. For they show impressively that for Luther the admonition to lead a true monastic life seamlessly connects with those approaches which he will identify as the core of his reformist breakthrough in the great retrospect of 1545. Fragments of letters to the Premonstratensian provost Georg Mascow in Leitzkau near Zerbst tend in the same direction.

The situation of one of these fragments is determined by Luther's experience of the plague, which, he says, indiscriminately destroys humans and cattle and which, by the sighs of mortal creatures, recalls to consciousness our sins and our misery, even though it should really be understood as a sign of grace rather than of wrath. Given the background of the Epistle to the Romans, the experience of a progressive deterioration can readily be explained as the expression of the *peccator fieri.* For only if we "become sinners" by recognizing as "sin" our incapacity for a loving fulfillment of the law, do we receive in faith the "justice of Christ" and can then live through that justice.

It is clear that, in spite of his later negative decision, Luther also understood his monasticism without reservation and qualification as the imitation of Christ, which is the reason why his life as friar was no delusion even though he and his friends later viewed and portrayed it as such.

4. FROM FRIAR TO REFORMER

We are now finally in a position to answer the question what one should make of Luther's spiritual assaults and struggles in the monastery. What was their nature, and what significance do they have in Luther's development as a reformer?

When one judges these phenomena objectively and fairly, one will discover that Luther's crises did not transcend the limits of the normal, were not caused by the monastic life style as such, and could have been resolved inside the monastery.

It is only the problem of "pure love" that requires clarification. The problem had its origin in Luther's practice of confession. It seems that absolution in Erfurt required "contrition" as the precondition for the effective remission of sins. In contrast to his fellow friars to whom the practice of confession caused no problems in this respect, this becomes an oppressively excessive demand for Luther. He cannot rouse the required contrition, certainly not by his own power, nor even through grace or the virtue of the love that is "infused" in our heart through justifying grace. The reason for the failure is Luther's conviction that he must feel and experience contrition as a determining power in his heart, as the expression of a surrender that is owed God, that cannot be replaced by compromise and especially not by the imperfect "gallows repentence" (attrition) which repents of sins merely because it wants its heavenly reward and is fearful of punishment in hell or purgatory. The ultimately unsuccessful though arduous attempt to "rouse" such contrition became the source of further insights and led to a problematic that extended beyond confession and the celebration of the mass.

To the extent that the fundamental question clearly became a problem for Luther alone, and to the extent that his otherwise excellent confessors and spiritual guides could not help the troubled friar in his distress, the question shows that Luther's case is unusual after all and ultimately comes to take on considerable significance. Concretely, this means that for the friars at the Erfurt Augustinian monastery, Luther's was not merely a singular but an alien problem that neither arose nor could readily be dealt with within the framework of the contemporary piety, spirituality, and theology of monasticism.

But while recognizing the distinctive character of the case, one will have to guard against exaggerations. For although the Catholicism of the period saw the problem of "pure love" as something strange, it was not wholly unknown nor, more importantly, a demonstrably un-Catholic problem. Instead, it is rooted in Holy Scripture, emerges in certain Fathers and saints, occasionally preoccupies mysticism and mystics, and disquiets theologians and especially the teaching of the Church. Generally speaking, one may call the problem a kind of borderline case whose riskiness makes one shrink back from it but which keeps returning and arises especially where the totality and the distinctive quality of a life in faith and as an imitation of Christ is concerned. But this also means that there is nothing about monasticism that would as a matter of principle have made impossible a Catholic solution of this problem even though it is true that Luther found no help in Erfurt.

This provides us with an important premise as we answer the second question, that is, what Luther's monastic battles meant for his development as a reformer. For if, in the majority of cases, Luther's difficulties can be defined as normal crises even though they occasionally became quite acute, and if his special problem had no monastic cause, we may begin our answer with a negative observation of considerable import, for now it may be taken as established that monasticism was not the cause of Luther's failure and that therefore Catholic monasticism must not be viewed as the dark background from which

Luther detached and freed himself in a painful process, or that he developed in a "reformist" direction as a result of this negative influence.

This thesis will initially surprise and confuse the reader. For if not this development, then what did make Luther the "reformer" whom we admire or criticize? But what appears so certain to us that we consider all further questions superfluous can quite easily and persuasively be shown to be less so. For if it was really this development that caused Luther to become a "reformer," why then did he not simply leave the monastery after he had developed his fundamental approach? Why does he, alone and deserted, continue on in the Black Cloister in Wittenberg until 1523 although the large majority of his fellow friars had long since decided in favor of the freedom of the gospel. Were they more "reformist" than the "reformer?" And what, finally, was the "reformist" element and the cause of the Reformation as we know it if Luther could develop its essential foundations as a friar and without encountering resistance when we consider that he publicly defended them before his order at the Heidelberg chapter in 1518, even after initial criticisms had set in?

Above, we briefly addressed the question of "pure love" in its original context, in connection with the contrition that must be awakened during confession. Now we must show how, in the course of theological reflection, the original question necessarily takes on greater amplitude. Anyone who, like Luther, attempts constantly and through the use of all of his or her powers and yet in vain to "mobilize" the requisite act of contrition will soon be confronted by the disturbing question whether the will has any power over the love of the heart at all or, more fundamentally still, whether the will to love is already love. We are taken a little further when we critically examine the reassuring information that we have the virtue of "infused love" through the sacramentally mediated justifying grace and that we abide "in this love" as long as we obey the commands and prohibitions of the law in what we do. The individual who, like Luther, judges such love to be insufficient because it allows the heart to be very far from God, and who thinks through the same question in terms of the Pauline theology of the law, is swept into a veritable vortex of extremely difficult theological problems: if only love can fulfill the law, what about the works of the law? Are they simply useless or even harmful because a mere façade of fulfillment of the law? But if works are necessary as an expression of a loving surrender to God, how does one become *voluntarius ad legem,* that is,

how does one find one's way to that spontaneous and gladdening "willingness" of a love that engenders its works as a tree its fruit?

If only love fulfills the law, then it alone is that "righteousness" which man cannot manufacture through works but which, in its entirety, must be God's gift so that we might live through and finally in it before and with God. But if God's love for us and our love for God and neighbor liberates us from all terror and all law, then love is identical with the "freedom of a Christian" which Luther demanded time and again, a freedom that liberates us from servitude to sonship and through love then makes us freely take upon ourselves the "form of a servant" in the discipleship of free obedience to our "self-emptying" Lord.

But if the love that fulfills the law and frees us is identical with our righteousness before God, Luther can understand the nature of unrighteousness and sin only in this context. If sin is ultimately the refusal of or incapacity for the total surrender to God in love, then venial sin also separates us from God, for it represents a guilty lessening of such love. There also occurs a shift in accent and a change in the evaluation of sin: the serious sins of those who stray from the path toward the "left" appear as much less serious than the "secret sins" of the Pharisees who stray toward the "right" and fall. For no one disputes the sinfulness of murder, adultery, and theft whereas it is only with difficulty that the objective fulfillment of the law that is guided by a pathological love is recognized as sin. Man's sin is greatest when, in view of all his virtues and achievements and in the enjoyment of his own virtuousness, he comes to feel that, through his fulfillment of the law, he has attained that perfection of love to which God owes the reward of heaven. The person who lives and acts from this conviction desecrates the "highest good," for he misuses the omnipotent God Himself in using Him as a means to his own blessedness. It is against this background that Luther's frequently misunderstood and easily misunderstandable, rather pointed phrases must be seen which, to the annoyance of the devout, inform us that it is precisely the "good works" of the Christians that should be feared as "mortal sins."

This context allows us to show what Luther means when he keeps calling on us to "sin bravely," when he opens our eyes to the mystery of "abiding sin," or represents the justification of man through God as the "becoming a sinner" which then leads to the seemingly so problematical definition of righteousness as being "simultaneously a sinner and justified." For in these somewhat confusing phrases, it is precisely not sins that cry to the heavens nor the "secret plague" of a perfection in "love" that has been achieved on one's own that are at stake. All that is involved here is the sin that can only be recognized through faith and that consists in the fact that even under and in the grace of God, we are still in no position to offer God the love we owe Him. But it must be seen that with the recognition and confession of this failure as "sin," man's situation has already fundamentally changed as far as Luther is concerned, for as we accept God's judgment that we are sinners and do so contrary to all appearance and contrary also to our self-estimate, the creative power of His word declares us to be just and there begins the real justification and, along with it, the strengthening and recovery of our sick love which attains perfection in and through death.

If this is so, Luther accomplishes through his *simul justus et peccator* a revaluation of sin as *felix culpa.* Then God transforms the "sin that dominates us" into the "sin we dominate" where our incapacity which we experience as sin brings us the community with Christ who has become sin for us and who through his cross as sacrament leads us, as "fellow crucified," to resurrection and the birth of the "new man."

It would now have to be shown that Luther found the answer to the vexing question about love in the cross of Christ, and this is the reason his theology of love has his theology of the cross as its immediate precondition. We understand that in the cross of His son, God hides Himself and His work and also His love and grace under their opposite. Whoever begins to live out of the mystery of divine love necessarily experiences the freely given and flowing love of God as the crucifixion of his miserable human love which only seeks itself and even on the cross does not lose sight of it. But what is hidden under the concealing veil of the opposite is already present for faith and promotes salvation.

If, throughout life, the Christian does not attain that perfect love that is owed God on the one hand, and if Luther understands faith not only as the devout acceptance of divine revelation but primarily as the obedient and confiding surrender of man to God on the other, it seems plausible that Luther should associate perfect faith with an as yet imperfect love. Such a nexus seems to make sense because, according to Scripture, there is a connection. Thus Luther thinks he is justified in saying that through its devotion "cheerful faith" anticipates the spontaneous "joy" of love and thereby promotes its growth. From the perspective of his theology of the cross, there is profound meaning in the statement that the devotion of faith conceals the devotion of love and also takes its place until the love of God has attained perfection. It makes profound sense when in view of his still feeble and sick love, the Christian can at least be certain in his belief in its perfection.

Yet in saying, "we put faith in the place of love"—the central phrase from the great commentary on the Epistle to the Galatians (1531)— Luther clearly goes too far, for here faith not merely "represents" love but "replaces" or "drives" it from the position which, according to Scripture and the tradition of the Christian religion including Luther, it deserves. The former "queen" is demoted to "servant girl" whose commerce henceforth is no longer with God but only with man. Driven from the king's "bridal chamber," she no longer lives from the devotion of her heart but torments herself under the constraint of the law in order to serve man through its works. This new ranking of love which demonstrably contradicts the unchanged fundament of Luther's theology unfortunately had historical effects. For already his contemporaries and even more those who came after him referred to Luther's polemical stratagem as "reformist" and were finally even proud to have sent "Catholic *caritas*" into the washhouse and the cowbarn.

If my thesis is correct, Luther's very own theology and the fundamental question that gives it its form and impetus can be claimed by neither the "Catholic" nor the "Reformist" creed of the period although the command that God be loved is of course as binding in the papal church as it is in the churches of the Reformation. What is exciting about Luther is that he bursts the framework of the old church without thereby leaving it, and that he does not establish a "new church" whose "reformist configuration" would be a function of its rejection of Catholicism. From this perspective, the uncommon and pronounced ecumenical potential of Luther's fundamental concerns becomes apparent. A person who goes along with Luther's questions and accompanies him on Abraham's path will quickly realize that in Luther also he has found a "father in the faith."

If my approach is correct, it also contains perfectly concrete insights that correct present judgment about Luther and the Reformation. For henceforth we will neither be able to maintain that in its form as monasticism the Catholic faith had been overcome by Luther once and for all and been replaced by the Reformed. Nor is the opposite thesis tenable according to which the Catholicism Luther overcame within himself was not Catholic at all, or that he heretically rediscovered for himself important elements of the Catholic faith. This is not to say that these theses are radically false. Indeed, they were and are unavoidable preliminaries to a real encounter with Luther. But where we do encounter him and engage his problems, and where, on our common path, we are suddenly beset by the question whether we might not be able to grasp Luther's faith as the possibility of our own, a line of demarcation which we considered impassable heretofore is suddenly crossed. The insight that occurs at that moment has direct consequences which also affect our presentation. For if the implicit assumption concerning the fundamental irreconcilability of the two creeds does not correspond to Luther's development and his fundamental theological concerns, the question about the contents of the Reformed faith also falls by the wayside, as does the question concerning the time at which Luther recognized and experienced it in a liberating breakthrough.

Of course, there also arises this new question: How can the course of the Reformation, troublesome to this very day, be explained? For if we may and must make it our point of departure that Luther's theological concerns do not compellingly account for the direction of the Reformation, then it is historical reasons that significantly determine its tragic course.

III

1. THE INDULGENCE CONTROVERSY AS OVERTURE TO THE CONTROVERSY WITH THE PAPAL CHURCH

Luther's theological position required clarification in two principal directions: vis-à-vis the Scholastic theology of the period, especially the Erfurt theology which had had some influence on him. But it also required clarification vis-à-vis the reformist-theological approaches of humanism which, under Erasmus, was advancing to the status of a European power in the intellectual realm of the time.

In the first of these two instances, Luther clarified his position principally as part of his teaching activity in Wittenberg, as is true of most professors. More than in the lectures themselves, such clarification expresses itself in the promotion disputations of his first students. After the course of lectures on the Epistle to the Romans, one such climax unquestionably occurs on September 25, 1516, during the promotion of Bartholomäus Bernhardi from Feldkirch. It was in the course of a disputation on "Man's Capacity for Salvation without Grace." The disputation theses deny to man any capacity for salvation apart from, or without, grace. They not only testify to the shaping influence of Paul but also evoke Augustine's authority to counter Scholasticism.

The reactions to the Bernhardi disputation on the part of his Wittenberg colleagues Petrus Lupinus and Karlstadt were sharp. Before an intensive study of Augustine induced Karlstadt to change his position radically, a rather violent dispute with Luther took place on the indulgence question. For when Karlstadt maintained that one would have to confess in the church of All Saints if one wished to obtain the indulgence granted there, and Luther promptly rejected this claim because he felt it hurt the Wittenberg ministry and the parish principle, the easily excited Karlstadt threatened to institute proceedings against Luther for being a "heretic" and ignoring a papal privilege. But before he could make good on this threat, Karlstadt had converted to Augustine, the decisive impetus being his study of *De spiritu et litera* which he edited and commented upon. He now prepared himself to do battle in behalf of Augustine and Wittenberg theology. On April 26, 1517, when the relics were exhibited in the Wittenberg castle church, Karlstadt affixed 151 theses to the church portal. They were to be disputed for a period of several days by theologians chosen by the elector.

The position that newly obtained in Wittenberg is unmistakably sounded when Luther writes to Johann Lang in Erfurt on May 18: "Our theology and Augustine are happily progressing and rule at our university through God's doing. Aristotle is declining and will soon disintegrate into a ruin. The traditional lectures on the *Sentences* disgust the students. No one can hope for listeners unless he lectures on the new theology, that is, on the Bible or Augustine or some other teacher with ecclesiastical authority."

In view of this situation, it is tantamount to a programmatic statement when, on the occasion of Franz Günther's promotion to baccalaureus biblicus on September 4, 1517, Luther calls for a disputation *contra scholasticam Theologiam* ("against Scholastic theology").

The élite of Protestant Luther scholars who search for what is genuinely "reformist" maintain that neither theses nor lectures contain "the program of a new theology but [merely] a settling of accounts with the misguided Aristotelianism of traditional Scholasticism" (M. Brecht). This misjudgment is understandable since they fail to recognize the constructive significance this fundamental question has for Luther's theology. It can be conceded, of course, that Luther has not yet extended his questions to include the relationship between love and faith or other significant themes such as sacrament, office, and church.

But before the disputation (which eventually takes place in Leipzig) becomes a possibility, Luther wants at least to defend his *Paradoxa* before his order at the Heidelberg chapter of the Reformed Congregation, in April 1518.

On this occasion, a young Dominican, Martin Bucer, will listen to him enthusiastically and congratulate him on a theology that strikes him as "Erasmian" through and through. It is understandable why many contemporaries should have had this impression, for there is an abundance of common elements and key terms, from the common front against Scholasticism to the preference for paradoxical formulations and the program of a renewal of theology for which Scripture and the Church Fathers would be the source.

Luther felt great urgency to defend his "new theology"

before the academic and ecclesiastical publics of contemporary theology. Quite differently from the way he had wished, he suddenly found himself in the limelight of history after presenting as a basis for a future disputation ninety-five theses on the meaning of indulgence to the competent bishops and his colleagues on the eve of All Saints' Day, 1517. That he affixed his theses to the portal of the Wittenberg castle church as Karlstadt had allegedly done before him has been disputed with good though not incontrovertible reason. There can be no doubt, however, that the image of a "hammer-wielding and zealous Luther" belongs to the realm of legend, however difficult it may be for devout churchgoers to surrender an idea they have come to cherish.

The indulgence problem, which Luther initially confronted in the confessional when his penitents importuned him with the "indulgence letters" of the great plenary indulgence which were being sold in Jüterbog or Zerbst by Johann Tetzel, required exhaustive treatment. With a frightening matter-of-factness, Pope Leo X and Albrecht of Brandenburg, cardinal archbishop of Mainz (as well as of Magdeburg and Halberstadt), had proposed to draw on the "inexhaustible treasures of Christ and the Church" to finance the construction of St. Peter's Basilica in Rome and to pay off Albrecht's "pious debts," 43,000 gulden in dispensation fees (for the illegal accumulation of benefices) and in pallium tax, which had been financed by the banking house of Fugger.

Much more important than yet another disquisition on that hoary topic, the traffic in indulgences and all its details—be its object to arouse a pious indignation or to loyally defend the Church—is, from my point of view, the rarely raised and even more rarely correctly answered question: How had this growth of indulgences been possible at all in God's Church, and what did it mean for the faith and the life of that Church?

Against the background of the history of penance, it becomes easy to identify all the characteristics of the system of medieval indulgence.

1. Indulgences derive from the pagan Germanic principle of restitution and are based on the endeavor to work off the temporal punishment due to sins by the smallest possible effort.

2. The orthodox and exemplary practice of the early Church of "intercession" and "vicarious penance" by the "confessor" or the "community" gave rise to the cruder notion of a "substitute penance" that was soon associated with the inexhaustible "treasure of the Church."

Title page of the papal bull *Exsurge Domine* of 1520, which threatened Luther with excommunication.

3. In connection with an intrinsically correct idea, the "temporal" punishment for sins that must be atoned for in time, the calculations of the penance tariff led to the childish and un-Christian quantification of the grace of indulgence.

4. It is in keeping with the Germanic principle of restitution that it became perfectly natural to commute the original works of piety for financial obligations: money, gold, or other valuables.

This summarizes the most important errors, though by no means all, of the practice of indulgence which, theoretically, was elaborated with the help of theologians, and this brings us to the theory of the matter. In the early Middle Ages, remissions were at first very modest—a matter of forty or eighty days. On the occasion of the consecration of churches or chapels, they were granted by bishops to those who, as donors or in other ways, had made possible their construction. There was thus a morally sustainable relationship between penitential works and the remission of temporal punishments which was always distinguished from the remission of eternal punishment when sins were forgiven in sacramental penance. But as in the course of time indulgences increased significantly and the relationship between them and works of piety became unclear, difficulties arose for those who administered penance. Theology was consulted and judged correctly that when pious works were not performed, that deficiency would have to be made up for by the person who had granted excessive remission, namely the father confessor or the bishop. But because, in the meantime, armies of praying monks had awakened the consciousness and the need of a Christian community that had persisted in its Germanic modes of feeling and argument, "substitute penance" soon proved inadequate. But in this unsuitable approach, the theologians with their razor-sharp distinctions discovered the possibility of an ever more perfect solution. For to move from "substitute penance" to the inexhaustible "treasure of Christ and his saints" which had been left to the pilgrim Church for its benefit did not prove a difficult expedition. Theology, ready to serve here as always, resolved the problem to the total satisfaction of all concerned: the "treasure of Christ," which was inexhaustible as a matter of principle, distributed with unerring certainty by the pope as the possessor of the highest power of the keys, was the theologians' seemingly ideal answer.

In one's criticism, one will have to guard against pious indignation and the zealous attempt to anticipate God's final judgment. It is the great advantage of Luther's theses on indulgence that they avoid such radical criticism. He knows indulgence too well "from the inside" and from the perspective of the medieval Christian. He knows that the lovingly assembled and exhibited collection of relics of his prince does not serve exclusively or even principally the making of money. He also knows that payments in the form of alms can assuredly express true penance, that the office of the keys must also administer penance judicially, and that we must represent each other before God, in prayer or by intercession, precisely as Christ interceded for us. But all this understanding does not calm Luther or make of him one of those apologists who contented themselves with defending the correctness of the practice of in-

dulgence and simply advocated that it be cleansed of its worst abuses. Instead, he senses in and behind the contemporary traffic in indulgences what made it, directly or indirectly, a lethal danger to the faith and the life of the Church.

Given these facts, little is gained by the unquestionably correct assertion that the forgiveness of sins and of the eternal punishments those sins incur could only be achieved by a contrite and valid confession, and that despite all abuses, intercession for the "poor souls" retained its Christian meaning.

It is certainly to Luther's credit not to have used the pope's and the archbishop of Mainz's horrendous dealings with the Fuggers as the basis for a radical attack on the old Church. The letter to Albrecht of Brandenburg refrains from any polemical allusion to this matter, and where the theses mention the building of St. Peter's or the huckstering practice of indulgence sermons, his arguments do not lack respect for the pope, nor does his sharp criticism make him forgetful of his love for the Church. Justifiably, he recalls the nature of true penance as Christ demanded it, a penance that extends to life in its entirety and cannot be discharged by a few works. Ingeniously if not with total clarity, he points to the inner connection between purgatory and the necessary purification of love. Carefully and relevantly, he reminds his addressee of the limits of papal power in the granting of remission, especially remission for the dead. Cautiously, he brings up the problematical "treasure of the Church" which is being put to such cavalier use. Irrefutably, he underlines in a sequence of theses the absolute primacy of "good works of love" over all remissions. For the "works of love" not only serve the neighbor in his need but also make man "better" and "increase" love while indulgence at best frees us from "punishment."

But from another point of view, Luther's meritorious criticism had a decisive effect on him and the renewal he aspired to, and this precisely because it was well founded. For the theses revealed the neuralgic points of the problematic of the medieval system of indulgences and thus compelled the sick Church of the period to take a position which, being involved in the indulgence traffic, it could not adopt unless it wished to run the risk of capitulation.

The correctness of this assertion can easily be demonstrated by the unfortunate course the discussion took. For although without Luther's knowledge and intent, the new medium of the printing press spread the theses throughout Germany with the speed of a forest fire, the reaction was initially unusually restrained: a disputation may have been planned but none took place. While many colleagues secretly agreed with Luther, there was no lack of adversaries either. Even Karlstadt was not in favor of a radical criticism of indulgences, and the theological faculties needed time as they always do or reacted with summary opinions when they were obliged to do so, as was the case of the faculty in Mainz. The bishops Luther had addressed did not actually react with unfriendliness or nervousness but were initially stumped. Only the archbishop of Mainz had to take a position. The advisers in Aschaffenburg instituted the *processus inhibitorius,* the professors delivered themselves of "opinions," the archbishop "informed" Rome, and the pope became annoyed at all the German profundity and tried at first to act through the superior general of the Augustinian Hermits.

The first formal reactions come from Johann Tetzel and Johann Eck. Although the theses do not mention him by name, the indulgence commissioner felt the understandable need to defend himself; presumably he had to. He is as radical here as in his sermons: within three weeks, Luther will burn at the stake. But because Tetzel can take no official action against Luther, he tries at the academic level: on January 20, 1518, he starts a disputation in defense of indulgences at the University of Brandenburg in Frankfurt an der Oder. The theses had not been formulated by Tetzel but by the leading theologian at Frankfurt, Konrad Koch, called Wimpina. They propose to refute Luther's theses sentence by sentence. Unfortunately, they merely demonstrate an utter blindness to the problem Luther has raised.

Tetzel's personally motivated and theologically primitive apologia was not taken seriously by Luther or the academics and bishops. This changed in the spring of 1518 when the Ingolstadt professor Johann Eck who had been considered a friend of Luther's up to this moment entered the discussion. Eck was a passionate "disputant" and about to discover an extensive sphere for that passion in his actually very laudable defense of a Church that was as vulnerable as it was reviled. *Obelisci* is the name of the signs scholars had been using since antiquity to identify those sentences in a corrupted text that were to be expunged. Playing the superior professor, Eck gave this title to a dissertation that he had originally intended for the bishop of Eichstätt and in which he dealt with the theses of the Augustinian from distant Wittenberg whom he treats as a Hussite and heretic, an insolent, ignorant know-nothing and even a contemnor of the pope.

This unfair and unexpected attack annoyed and disappointed Luther. It is said that he originally intended not to pursue the matter but then, pressed by his friends, he decided to send the arrogant and excited professor a proper response which he would entitle *Asterisci* (little stars), a term used by scholars to designate the valuable parts of a text.

Here again, it was Karlstadt who saw to it that the next round would take place. Forgetting his earlier doubts about his colleague's excessively sharp critique of indulgences and interested in publicity, he published Luther's theses against the *Obelisci* without the author's knowledge, an event that Eck could not ignore.

2. A CARDINAL'S HAT OR THE STAKE: LUTHER ON TRIAL

Before going on to Eck's successful attempt to lure Luther into the arena at Leipzig, we will report briefly how the quarrel continued and proceedings in Rome were instituted against Luther. Already at this point, it is clear that these actions may perhaps lead to a condemnation but certainly not to a clarifying decision.

After the interlude of the Heidelberg chapter before which Luther was allowed to defend the fundamental concerns, the *Paradoxa* of his theology of the cross, though not the indulgence question, he quickly prepared his extensive comment on the indulgence theses, the so-called *Resolutions,* for the printer. The document is preceded by a letter to Staupitz, whom he asks to transmit it to the pope, and a dedication to Leo X. In both letters, Luther is after the same thing: he defends his understanding of penance against the false interpretation by the Dominicans; he defends himself against the reproach that he has attacked the position of the pope, and acknowledges in his voice the voice of Christ, however the decision may turn out.

While Luther has Staupitz pass his resolutions on to the pope, proceedings against him have been instituted in Rome, and it is irrelevant whether this occurred with or without Dominican help. Marius de Perusco, the papal finance official who was charged with the prosecution of the case, requested that Luther be put on trial. Leo X called on the court theologian Sylvester Prierias, a Dominican, to write a theological opinion, and charged the bishop Hieronymus Ghinucci with the preliminary judicial investigation. It took no more than three days to com-

17   On December 10, 1520, Luther burns the papal bull *Exsurge Domine* before the Elster gate in Wittenberg. The bull, issued on June 15, 1520, threatened Luther with excommunication unless he recanted in sixty days. Shortly thereafter, the works of the "heretic Luther" were banned in Burgundy by the newly elected emperor Charles V, and in October and November of 1520 Luther's books were burned in Louvain, Lüttich, Cologne, and Mainz.—Colored Woodcut from the "History" of Ludwig Rabus (1557). Wittenberg, Lutherhalle.

18   Martin Luther before the emperor at the Diet of Worms. On April 17, 1521, Luther was called on to recant his writings in the bishop's residence. On April 18, he refused to recant before the emperor "because to do something against one's conscience is neither safe nor salutary. May God help me. Amen."—Colored woodcut.

19   The imperial document by which Emperor Charles V outlawed Martin Luther who left Worms on April 26, 1521, under the escort of the imperial herald Caspar Sturm. The reading and diffusion of his writings had been placed under severe penalties. After hearing Luther, Charles V declared: "Henceforth, I will view him as a notorious heretic."—Secret Vatican Archives.

20   Charles V, German emperor from 1519, whom Luther faced at the Diet of Worms on April 17 and 18, 1521. The emperor, who saw it as incumbent on himself to commit "all his realms, friends, his body and his blood, his life and his soul" to the preservation of the Catholic faith and the Catholic Church, could only view Luther as a heretic whom, along with his followers, he saw it his duty to fight.—Painting by Barent van Orley (around 1521), Budapest.

Edict Keyserlic/buptghegheuen by kaerle den viifsten Ghecozen keysere
des Roomschē rycke/Altijts des rijcs vermeerdere/Coninc Catholijck ꝛc
int zeer vmaerde verzamen des helics Rijcke/te Woozms/int iaer ons hee
ren duust vijfhondert ende een en twintich.

❡ Ieghēs bzoeder Marti luther vā sente Augustyns oozdene vweckere
der oude en vwesene ketteriē/en heresiē/en der nieuwer en voozthzighere

❡ Ieghens alle de bouckē oder Luthers name buptghegheuē/en die naer
maels buptghegheuē zullē werden/en der zeluer boucken van nv voozt an
Pzenters:coopers: en vercoopers.

❡ Ieghens Luthers mede zweerers/onthauders/of bedeckers en die hem
ionste draghen in wat manieren dat het zy.

❡ Ieghens opspzakelicke en famoise libellen of boucken Oec ieghens
beilden of seilderien van dier manieren/ende harer butgheuers: pzenters
coopers: ende vercoopers van wat name of condicien zy zyn.

❡ Statupt ende wet den pzenters/om te belettene en te vbiedene tquaet
dwelke daghelics ghebuert by den mesbzupcke der louelicker conste van
pzentene.
❡ De Peynen.

❡ Van Cryme lese maieste.grotelic te mesdoene ieghen des Keysers ghe
bodt/ende z waerlic te ballene in zynder indignacie.

❡ Up confistatie ende verbuerte van lisue ende van allen goede wat het
zy vaste of roerelic/waer af deen helft cōmen zal der keyserlicker maiesteit
ende de andre den anbzynghere of wzoughere. Bouen andre peynen
inde rechten begrepe/alzoot bzeeder blyct in die ieghē wozdich edict.

Vorrede
Der Prophet
Jeremia.
XXXVI.
I.
SODOM,
PHARAO
JERVSA-
LEM.

21   Elector Frederick the Wise (1463—1525) was Luther's prince and protector. On December 18, 1518, he refused, in a letter to the papal Curia, to surrender Luther to the authorities in Rome, and commented as follows: "If we were convinced that his teaching is impious and untenable, we would not defend him. It is our sole intent to fulfil the office of a Christian prince."—Detail of the bronze epitaph of the elector in the Wittenberg castle church by Peter Vischer the Younger (1527).

22   Martin Luther as "Junker Jörg." Returning from the Diet of Worms, Luther was "attacked" by Electoral-Saxon horsemen near Eisenach on May 9, 1521, and taken to the Wartburg where he lived in this disguise until the spring of 1522. In a letter to Spalatin, he wrote: "I had to wear a horseman's garb and let my hair and beard grow so that you would scarcely recognize me."—Painting (1521) by Lucas Cranach the Elder. Weimar, State Collection in the castle.

23   Luther's study at the Wartburg where, from 1521—1522, he translated the New Testament into German. The first publication of three thousand copies, an enormous number for the period, came out in September 1522.

24   On the table of the Luther room at the Wartburg lies a copy of the second edition of Luther's complete translation of the Bible which was printed in Wittenberg in 1541 by Hans Lufft. The pages of the book contain corrections and marginalia by Luther and Melanchthon.

plete his opinion—an excessively speedy procedure that will cause some unhappiness later—and he submitted it to the court in early June. In August 7, the cardinal legate Thomas de Vio, better known as Cajetan, who was in Augsburg at the time, sent Luther the summons which called on him defend himself in Rome within sixty days.

How Rome conceived of the proceedings becomes clear from Prierias' *Dialogue on the Power of the Pope against Luther's Theses,* which was handed to the accused along with the summons. Summarizing the argument that was designed either to make Luther recant or to burn him at the stake, we formulate as follows: the pope is the highest and infallible teacher of the Church in all questions of faith and morals. Indulgences are part of this. Anyone who attacks or questions indulgences therefore questions or disputes the power of the pope and is consequently a heretic. What was new here but plausible was the constant invocation of Thomas Aquinas as "teacher of the Church."

Suddenly, events follow each other in rapid succession. After a papal brief of August 23 to the legate, the summons is withdrawn because the preliminary investigations are practically complete. The cardinal is to seize this friar who has been recognized as a notorious heretic and to keep him in custody until the end of the proceedings. Only if Luther should appear voluntarily before the cardinal and humbly ask to be forgiven for his boldness is Cajetan empowered to readmit the contrite sinner into the Church. Should he refuse, Cajetan is to excommunicate him and his adherents and to break all resistance with the punishments canonical law provides.

Concurrent attempts to induce the elector to withdraw his protection or to induce the heads of the order to surrender Luther do not produce the desired result.

Beginning in late August, politics, that is, Emperor Maximilian's plan to have himself elected king, changed the situation and placed Luther in a more favorable position. The legate needed the elector and, on September 11, Rome softened its instructions: Cajetan is now given the power to summon Luther and to accept his recantation or to condemn him. But he must not involve himself in a disputation.

Being a theologian of some standing and extremely conscientious, the legate read Luther's writings and composed a number of tracts on the questions they raised. Without changing the theological framework of the questions, he directed conversation to two points he considered central: he believed he had discovered the decisive difference concerning the doctrine of justification in Luther's thesis on the certainty of faith (and this has been the view of controversial theology to this day), and he followed Aquinas in viewing the doctrine of the "treasure of the Church" as the basis for the papal power of granting indulgences.

Ordered to Augsburg by Frederick the Wise, Luther finally makes his appearance on October 7. In spite of considerable efforts by both sides, the interrogation does not have a good result. Because an attempt at a written apology does not fulfill the expectations of the cardinal, Luther appeals to the "pope who must be more adequately informed" and leaves town precipitately on the evening of October 20. Back in Wittenberg, he intends to appeal to the future council. But the question whether the pope himself might not be the Antichrist takes on an ever increasing urgency for him.

Before matters escalate, an important interlude occurs. Emperor Maximilian, the "last knight," dies in January 1519. Settling the imperial succession becomes the principal preoccupation of papal politics and Frederick the Wise the key figure in the process. The pope, concerned about the papal state and its destiny here on earth, momentarily forgets about "temporal punishments," his "power of indulgence," and the "notorious heretic" in distant Wittenberg. For a period of almost twenty months, the heresy trial is interrupted. During this time, the "poor souls" and the Church enjoy a respite and Luther can breathe a sigh of relief and work with superhuman energy to fulfill his tasks as preacher and professor.

This interlude is filled by two contradictory events that cut across each other in time. The first is associated with Karl von Miltitz, the second with the passionate disputant Johann Eck.

The first event is part of the political deal papal diplomacy tried to strike with the Saxon elector. Karl von Miltitz, chamberlain and secretary of Pope Leo X, came from the lesser Saxon nobility and was acquainted with the elector through his father. In discharging himself of his mission, Junker Karl did in fact prove skillful. He deposited the Golden Rose, the papal decoration he was to offer Frederick the Wise, in the Fugger's safe before setting out on his good will journey to Nuremberg and Altenburg. At the various stops, the hospitably received nuncio informed himself until far into the night of what the Germans were thinking. At the same time, he revealed to his astonished countrymen how people in the highest places in Rome actually felt about Luther.

As is customary in diplomacy, the elector used the compliant chamberlain, of course, inasmuch as his reports and offers were more than opportune, considering that in December he, the elector, had told Cajetan definitively that he would not surrender Luther since the Wittenberg professor had not been proved guilty of heresy, was open to correction, and always ready to dispute. It was none other than Karl von Miltitz (not Cajetan) who, acting on the orders of the pope to win Frederick the Wise's assent to the plan regarding the imperial election, was to advise the elector, in a clearly official manner, that one of his friends might be made a cardinal. Although from the very beginning the chamberlain's plan to move the case of Luther out of the realm of politics and into that of church discipline had no chance of success (Luther had already called the pope the "Antichrist"), the papal image that emerges from Luther's letter is certainly not inaccurate nor, more importantly, insignificant. For it shows how the "Holy Father" and the sincerely pitied, "most miserable Leo" might never have become the "Antichrist" for Luther in the first place. As regards Luther himself, it is a historical fact that because of his understandable rejection of the bizarre and unlikable Saxon Junker, but especially through his dangerous overestimation of theology and doctrine, he contributed significantly to the failure of the plan.

Parallel to the Miltitz affair was the initiative of Eck, an event in which Luther as a theologian placed all his hopes. We have already suggested that Karlstadt's unexpected theses against Eck's *Obelisci* were the point of departure for the entire enterprise. But it is significant that Eck conducted the preparatory discussion concerning place and time of the disputation with Luther, not with Karlstadt. The twelve that Eck published in December 1518 on penance, indulgence, the treasure of the Church, and purgatory are addressed to Karlstadt but are actually directed at Luther, especially the twelfth (later the thirteenth) on the authority of pope and Church which again outlines the framework within which Luther was to be finally unmasked. In spite of his agreement with Miltitz not to preach, write, or discuss, Luther promptly answered with counter theses and proclaimed that he would participate in what became the famous Leipzig disputation from June 27 to July 16, 1519, to which Duke George admitted him at the last hour and as a result of Eck's intervention.

In the course of his hectic preparations, Luther develops insights regarding the problem of papal authority and indirectly also the authority of the councils. He tries to verify hitherto undisputed dogmatic propositions against the background of a very tempestuous history—an attempt that is far ahead of its time. In the course of this work, the papacy which jealousy protects and develops its power increasingly takes on the aspects of the Antichrist. Only someone with an intimate knowledge of the *Decretum Gratiani* and the papal "decretals" can judge what the intensive study of the newly opened sources must have meant for Luther's image of the pope. For what was he to think of a papacy that could see the spiritual predicament of the system of indulgences only from the point of view of its own prestige and tried to regulate by new decretals—such as the indulgence decretal of Leo X dated November 9, 1518—what could only be repressed and made more acute but never clarified by such a procedure. It is obvious that in this context the invocation of Scripture was the only defense against decrees, decretals, council resolutions, and theological propositions whose biblical grounding became an immense problem, and not only for Luther. It must also be conceded, however, that the scriptural principle that was thus being directed against the Church now assumed a significance it had not previously had for Luther and which it would not have attained without him.

A further comment on the Antichrist thesis that henceforth will orient Luther's quarrel with the papacy and which, especially in the final and crude polemical text, *Against the Roman Papacy, an Institution of the Devil* (1515), most Catholics find to be intolerably repugnant and heretical. Without wishing to excuse a crudeness that soon went beyond all bounds, we should not become so indignant that we forget the theological significance this terrible accusation has for Luther. For him, "Antichrist" is no insult but denotes, in the sense of 2 Thessalonians 2: 3–12, the "rebellion" that precedes the day of the Lord. The "man of lawlessness" and the "son of perdition" must be revealed who takes "his seat in the temple" to have himself worshiped as God. Luther takes this expression very seriously indeed, although some time passes before he becomes fully aware of all it entails. The following are the important insights here: the Antichrist and the rebellion he causes must become actual historical events, and the rebellion can occur only in God's temple, that is, within the "true Church." It does not manifest itself in the "sects" and thus becomes the indirect eschatological sign of the "true Church" though that Church does not lose what makes it the Church as a result of his advent. The Antichrist therefore changes the structure of the Church only

The seven-headed papal bull. Pamphlet against the traffic in indulgences.

tors choose the new emperor in Frankfurt, the Wittenbergians come to Leipzig where Eck, confident of victory, is already expecting his adversaries.

On July 4, at seven o'clock in the morning, Eck finally encounters Luther, whom he had really wanted to dispute, rather than Karlstadt. Eck, the matador and passionate disputant, does not succeed in teaching, let alone convincing, the Wittenberg friar. But he does goad Luther into making statements about the primacy of the pope, the capacity for error of councils as in the case of Hus, and Scripture as the sole source of faith. The depressing result is that Luther's great hope is not fulfilled as might have been expected. The universities at Paris and Erfurt which had been selected as judges refrain because the threatening quarrel frightens them. Only the universities of Louvain and Cologne send two lame opinions months later which provoke the cutting answer from Luther that even those professors who conduct themselves as if they were infallible succumb to error.

It must be conceded, of course, that as provoked assertions and in the context of the situation described above, Luther's statements are not only misinterpretable, exaggerated, and onesided, but clearly "heretical" in their tendency. But all these defects do not result from the theological approach but can be explained by historical accidents. This is confirmed by the fact that the "heretical" element in Luther as we observe it in a crescendo movement in the three great programmatic tracts of 1520 is never unambiguous or definitive, let alone clearly "unCatholic." It can be shown further that the themes he dealt with in Leipzig or later—such as church office, the sacraments, the mass, or monasticism—could have been treated in a way that would have allowed for Luther's distinctive approach, yet been perfectly understandable as "Catholic."

This clearly applies not only to Luther but also to Eck and the other Catholic adversaries. It was more than simple passion that inspired Eck during the disputation and the prompt exploitation of its results. For we must assume that on the basis of Eck's dogmatically fixed and undeveloped doctrine of the Church it was quite simply a historical impossibility for him to understand the fundamental concerns behind the bold and equally immature and exaggerated pronouncements of the man from Wittenberg.

The entire further development is thus governed by a "historical necessity" which, in its human, all-too-human causes and the ambivalence of its motivations, never attained the stringency of "theological necessity," yet quite

in the sense that he dethrones God and takes his place, and it is this that constitutes the horror of the rebellion. Applied to the pope, this means that it is not through his position of power but through its misuse that is directed against God, or because his vicarship thrusts God out of the way, that he is the Antichrist. The ultimate consequence that has governed Luther's thought from the very beginning although its full significance only dawned on him gradually is this: the coming of the Antichrist means that the end of time has arrived. Even the Reformation therefore cannot prevent the "rebellion." Only the day of the Lord or the "beloved day of Judgment" as Luther hopefully calls it will bring salvation.

By way of anticipation, we have now also suggested what the Leipzig disputation will effect. While the elec-

concretely seized and directed the life of the faith and the church and of theological development.

If this is so, the further course of this sad story, from the writing of the bull threatening excommunication to the Diet of Worms and Luther's "kidnapping" to the Wartburg, can be condensed. We know the human qualities and weaknesses of the principal actors; we know the hopeless opposition between the two positions. A decision must be made, but, in the event, that decision will decide nothing.

With Eck's arrival in Rome on March 25, the proceedings entered a new phase. Because of his experience in Leipzig and coming from Germany, Eck knows more clearly than his Roman colleagues that more than indulgences are involved. Toward the end of April, a new commission is formed of which not only the two cardinals but Eck also are members. A bull against Luther is to be discussed, and to it Eck contributes those forty-one propositions that are no longer to be condemned one by one but globally. On May 2, Eck reports on the bull to Leo X. As always when commissions make decisions, not everyone is in agreement with the bull threatening excommunication. Before the substance of the forty-one propositions is subjected to a critique, Cajetan objects to the wholesale condemnation and the canonists register their dissatisfaction with the procedure. It is probable that they did not make too much of their real doubt which concerned the relationship between pope and council. The bull thus contains a number of distinctions and uncertainties that either go unrecognized or are quickly forgotten if one simply listens to the bombastic trumpet solo of the *Exsurge Domine* ("Arise, O God, plead thy cause," Psalm 74:??) with which the Medici pope called not only on God but on heaven and earth, and especially the emperor and the empire, for help against the "wild boar that wreaks havoc in the vineyard of the Lord."

The bull does not directly impose the ban and the unending list of canonical punishments, but Luther, the "notorious heretic," is given sixty days. The bull also distinguishes between person and doctrine and even between erroneous and non-erroneous books. There are additional indications whose actual significance can only be judged by those with a specialized knowledge of the papal chancery: the bull is dated June 15, and the signatures of the pope and the cardinals, which were so important to Eck and customary in the case of bulls, are missing. Instead of the appropriate seal-cord of hemp that protocol calls for, a multi-colored one is used; the proclamation

With this caricature of the seven-headed Martin Luther, Johann Cochläus, in a polemical writing of 1529, attacks the contradictory statements of his opponent.

date is July 24 when it is posted on the door of St. Peter's and in the papal chancery on the Campo dei Fiori.

Then—not without some concern for the reaction of the elector, who had told Aleander, the papal nuncio, as late as November that he would resent attacks by Luther on the pope—there occurred, on December 10, the famous scene before the Elster gate: called on by Melanchthon, students burned the hated papal decretals and scholastic books such as the *Summa Angelica*, and Luther —hardly noticed by those present—himself threw the bull into the fire.

The bull *Exsurge Domine*, being a theological and ecclesiastical judgment, cannot be so easily undone although this does not mean that the "highest judge" did not foresee a "revision" for such "contradictory judgments." And this revision which precedes the final judgment sets in when those responsible for the bull before history begin to see the "contrariety" of their judgment. In the present case, it is none other than Johann Eck himself who, having learned something from his experiences as the nuncio of the bull, admits in a reform opinion for Adrian VI the shortcomings of the old bull and demands a new one: in the old bull, he writes, much had remained obscure and many of the condemned propositions had been so trivial that even the greatest scholars could not understand why they should have been condemned. The urgently proposed "new" judgment should therefore confine itself to the most important errors and refute them by full recourse to Holy Scripture. It is a consolation that even the "passionate disputant" slowly discovered the capacity for instruction. Eck, however, never achieved a revision of the bull.

It was in fact this contradictoriness of the bull and of the entire procedure that defined the further course of negotiations. Having finally been proclaimed *haereticus vitandus* by the edict of excommunication *Decet Romanum Pontificem*, on January 3, 1521 (the date on which the friar who had been recognized as a "notorious heretic" for years was actually condemned is a purely theoretical matter) Luther should have been outlawed immediately according to prevailing secular and ecclesiastical law. For the implementation of the church ban was the business of the emperor as the secular arm of the Church. But it is legitimate to wonder why the emperor should have been less "ambivalent" than the pope and his judgment.

The emperor had important reasons not to make short shrift in Luther's case. Quite apart from the fact that the Germans almost unanimously backed Luther and opposed the Curia, a fact no one recognized and expressed more clearly than Aleander, the emperor also had to take the interests of the Diet into account. He could not overlook the fact that in the course of time Luther had become something like the "mouthpiece" for all the complaints of the German empire, that he had committed himself by a solemnly sworn election capitulation to outlaw no one without a previous hearing, and that he had finally promised Frederick the Wise to give Luther a fair hearing at the Diet which up to this time the condemned man had been unable to obtain.

Thus, although important concessions to the papal side are made, the emperor does not simply impose the ban. Instead, he summons Luther, sending along a safe conduct in which he addresses him as "honorable, dear and pious Martin," and asks that he give information about his books before the Diet. There is no mention of recantation.

On March 29, Kaspar Sturm, the imperial herald, himself highly critical of Rome, presented the summons to Luther in Wittenberg. As early as April 2, Luther set out on a journey which, because it could have been his last, initially proceeded like a triumphal procession. The town had presented him with a requisitioned dray equipped with a roof, and the university had allowed him expenses in the amount of twenty gulden. Although he had been expelled from the order, the monastery provided him with a companion as stipulated in its rules, the not terribly consequential Father Johann Fetzensteiner, and Luther even had his tonsure trimmed. Whereas his lectures obliged Melanchthon to stay behind, two other colleagues, Nikolaus von Amsdorf and a young nobleman from Pomerania, accompanied him. Pleasantly escorted by the herald, Luther journeyed through Germany's towns, where he was everywhere hospitably received.

Luther's mood wavered between fear and defiant confidence. According to Cochlaeus's believable report, he caroused with friends in Frankfurt, strumming his lute, an Orpheus in his cowl. But his popularity did not go to his head. Although the pronouncements he allegedly made on this journey are full of pathos, this odd friar was genuinely convinced of his mission and knew that Christ in whom he put his entire faith and love would protect him on his journey.

Although the two nuncios had tried to arrange as inconspicuous an arrival as possible, a solemn reception, which really should have been avoided, awaited him. On the morning of April 16, trumpets announced Luther's arrival from the cathedral. Thousands went out to see the man no one knew what to make of—reformer and liberator of the Church or "wild boar" that had crashed into the vineyard of the Lord. On practical grounds, Luther was taken to the friendly Knights of Rhodes who had once kept Prince Dschem for Alexander VI. Under the generous supervision of the elector's advisors and the imperial marshal who were put under the same roof, communication with Luther was no longer a problem.

The next morning, the details of the procedure were settled. Luther would be restricted to answering the questions addressed to him and not be allowed to make additional statements. He would appear before the Diet, in the episcopal palace next door to the cathedral, at four o'clock in the afternoon. Accompanied by the marshal and the imperial herald and led like a thief through the garden of the Knights of Rhodes and down a few back streets to the rear entrance of the episcopal palace, Luther finally stood before his emperor and the estates of the empire. According to Aleander who was not present, the "fool" was laughing, and others report that he "looked merry." Unfamiliar with court etiquette, Luther must have tried to spot familiar faces and is even supposed to have spoken briefly with C. Peutinger from Augsburg. The marshal then admonished him not to speak until and unless a question was addressed to him.

The archbishop's chancellor, Johann von Eck, functioned as the emperor's plaintiff. Facing the books that had been placed on a bench, the chancellor asked Luther in the name of the emperor and with reference to the summons whether he recognized the books as his, and whether he acknowledged them or wished to disavow parts of them. Although the questions allowed for a number of possible answers, Luther seemed frightened and confused. In a barely audible voice, he affirmed the first question and indicated briefly that he might have written more. As he answers the second, he suddenly loses his nerve. Whether he wished to avow or disavow, this second and decisive question suddenly strikes Luther as involving ultimate matters and—to the disappointment of his friends and the amazement of his adversaries—he humbly requests time to reflect.

When, on the next day and at the same time, he again faced the emperor and had to answer the second question, he calmly and resolutely took the cross of the ambiguous situation upon himself. Answering with a firm voice, he makes a three-fold distinction among his writings. He does not need to recant the first group which is devoted to his fundamental concerns because it is general and endorsed even by his adversaries. He cannot recant the writings in the second group, the polemics against the papacy, because the popes, invoking their "decretals," have acted against Scripture and the Church Fathers and made themselves the lords of Christendom. The third group includes those writings that are addressed to specific adversaries and with reference to which he concedes that stylistically,

The dream of Frederick the Wise at Schweinitz in 1517 on the outcome of the posting of the 95 Theses against indulgences. Luther recounts the dream in his *Table Talk*.

25 Martin Luther in the pulpit. Detail of the predella of the altarpiece in the town church in Wittenberg. Tradition reports that this masterpiece by Lucas Cranach the Elder was erected on April 24, 1547, the day of the Battle of Mühlberg in which Charles V defeated the troops of the Evangelical Schmalkaldic League. After his victory, on the Wednesday before Pentecost, the emperor marched into Wittenberg which had surrendered and visited Luther's grave in the castle church. When Charles V was called on to open the grave and to burn Luther's remains because he had been a heretic, he is reported to have answered: "I wage war against the living, not against the dead." But a Spanish officer from the emperor's retinue pierced the painting of the preaching Luther with his sword (at the neck and in the body), and shouted: "Even in death, this beast rages on." The holes made by the sword thrusts are visible still.

26 Peasants' War, the battle of Gaisbeuren (1525) near Ravensburg. Detail of the 1528 escutcheon of the town of Überlingen.—Überlingen, town hall.—The discontent of the German peasants about economic, social, and religious matters led to early unrest in 1493 under the banner of the "Bundschuh" movement along the Upper Rhine and in Württemberg (1514). When the movement spread, Luther first wrote his *Admonition to Peace on the Twelve Articles of the Swabian Peasantry* (1525). He protested the false understanding of the gospel by the peasants who proposed making a law of it and transforming it into a social reality by the use of violence. Only after his appeal had found insufficient resonance did he write *Against the Robbing and Murdering Mobs of Peasants,* in May 1525. He then called on the princes to exercise their right to the sword and to put an end to the peasants' uprising.

27, 28 Martin Luther and Katharina von Bora, painting (1526) by Lucas Cranach the Elder, Wartburg.— Katharina von Bora (* 1499) became a Cistercian nun in Nimbschen convent in 1515. During the night before Easter 1523, she secretly fled from the convent with eleven other nuns. Luther, who knew of and supported this escape, married Katharina on July 13, 1525.

29   View into the choir of the parish church of St. Mary in Wittenberg with altarpiece by Lucas Cranach the Elder (cf. no. 25). This altar, like the other great Reformation altars of Cranach's, is a demonstration of Luther's opposition to the iconoclasm of Karlstadt. In his *Against the Heavenly Prophets in the Matter of Images and Sacraments* (1525), Luther defended Christian art. In connection with the biblical illustrations to which the iconoclasts did not object, Luther wrote: "They should not begrudge us our painting such images on the wall so that we might remember and understand better since on walls they do no more harm than in books. I wish to God I could persuade the princes and the wealthy to have the entire Bible painted on the walls of houses so that everyone might see them. That would be a Christian work."

30   The Last Supper with the reformers as Christ's apostles. Altar painting for the castle church of St. Mary in Dessau, the last of the Reformation altars to be completed by Lucas Cranach the Younger, in 1565. The altarpiece, commissioned by Prince Joachim von Anhalt who, as the donor, is seen kneeling in the left foreground, shows on the left, next to Christ, his brother Georg, whom Luther had ordained in 1544 and of whom he had said: "Prince Georg is more pious than I am. If he should not enter heaven, I certainly won't." Next to him, we see Martin Luther, Johannes Bugenhagen, Justus Jonas, and Caspar Cruciger. To the right and next to Christ, seated, are Philip Melanchthon, followed by Johann Forster, Johann Pfeffinger, Georg Major, and Bartholomäus Bernhardi. In the background, standing, additional members of the house of Anhalt. In the right foreground, Lucas Cranach the Younger as cup bearer.

31   The congregation during the sermon. Detail of the predella of the town church altarpiece (cf. nos. 29, 25). The congregation, according to the Augsburg Confession, "is the gathering of all the faithful to whom the gospel is preached purely and the holy sacraments are administered in accordance with the gospel." Cranach also painted Luther's son Hänschen in this congregation. He is leaning against his mother's knee. The figure behind these two may be one of Luther's daughters.

if not in their substance, they may have been more vehement than necessary, a statement which clearly shows that he cannot recant the substance of any of them.

He then discusses the danger to the unity of the Church and emphasizes that he also is concerned with this unity but that it is not possible to avoid destructive tension where the Word of God is concerned, for Christ had come not to bring peace but the sword. It is therefore not at the expense of the Word but only through the Word itself that the conflict can be settled.

It was very hot in the room and Luther perspired profusely but he insisted on also presenting his statement in Latin. In his answer, the chancellor praised the emperor's patience but rejected Luther's statement as insufficient. As is customary in such situations, he finally demanded an honest and simple answer to what was anything but a simple question. Luther cannot and will not be evasive but even at this point he does not become the defiant hero people prefer to see. He certainly never spoke the words "Here I stand, I cannot do otherwise." They are legend. In actuality, Luther simply invoked his "conscience," though a conscience that has nothing whatever in common with the autonomous conscience of today. For Luther emphasizes again that he is prepared to be refuted by clear scriptural testimony and plausible rational grounds. Even here, he does not radically reject pope and councils as authorities although he does state that he cannot believe them "alone" since it is a historical fact that they have erred and contradicted themselves in the past.

The effort before the Diet which had been initiated with so much trouble had failed. The emperor, just as the Church before him, could not act otherwise. But neither could Luther. Despite all that was done, the estates did not succeed in getting Luther to change his mind during the three-day period the emperor had granted. On the evening of April 25, the emperor informs Luther that, everything having failed, he now must, as the protector of the Church, take steps against him.

It is one of the oddities of this story that the "Edict of Worms," which Aleander had prepared and the emperor had signed after the termination of the Diet on May 26, 1521, and which had finally banned and outlawed an "obvious heretic," had a merely indirect effect. For the outlawed Luther had already left, but certainly not escaped from, Worms, on April 26, with his escort. True, he was not sure what would happen next but he could have confidence in his God and his elector. With traveling money from the elector's treasury, a safe conduct from Philip of

Hesse, and a solemn farewell banquet, the "honest rascal" as Aleander called him sets out on a journey whose destination no one knows for sure. From Oppenheim on, the imperial herald and twenty horsemen, allegedly provided by Sickingen, escort him again. They travel via Frankfurt to Friedberg where he discharges the herald because he feels safe. He does not proceed directly from Eisenach to Gotha but, escorted only by Amsdorf and Petzensteiner, makes a detour to Möhra where he visits his relatives. As they set out from Möhra, it happens: on May 4, the small company is attacked by armed horsemen in a narrow passage near Altenstein castle. Amsdorf curses like a foot soldier, Petzensteiner saves himself by jumping into the bushes, and Luther has just time enough to pick up his New Testament and Hebrew Bible. Then, first on foot and later on horseback, they move by detours toward their secret destination. At eleven o'clock at night, Luther arrives at the safe Wartburg where, perfectly camouflaged as "Junker Jörg" and out of the public's eye, he will spend the following ten month praying, raging, and working. The elector was not only "wise" but also cunning when the situation called for it. The cleverly arranged maneuver succeeded, the witnesses kept silent, and the hoodwinked public soon spoke of a violation of the safe conduct that had cost Luther his life. Albrecht Dürer who was in the Netherlands at the time grieved for the dead Luther and the Bible that would fall silent now until God sent a new witness.

Generally believed dead, Luther works feverishly in his solitude, especially on the sample sermons, postils, and a translation of the New Testament. But as Junker Jörg who soon also roams the forests and the countryside, he seems to be moving in an ecclesiastical no-man's land. The old papal Church has expelled him and wants him dead whereas the "Church of the Reformation" is taking its first steps in Wittenberg and elsewhere without, and against, him. Yet paradoxically, he belongs to both churches, for he belongs to the Lord of the Church and, abandoning everything and ahead of everyone, he sets out in the faith of Abraham and his Church for the "Day of the Lord."

Frederick the Wise finds himself in a similar situation: in his heart and in his faith, he has long been traveling the road Luther is taking. But this does not prevent him from remaining in the train of the pilgrim Church, as it were. For in it, and in the belief that it also will set out, he wishes to serve as the rear guard of the man who is already on the way. We may also be certain that the elector was no less critical of the tempestuous beginnings of the Reformation in Wittenberg than Luther was himself even though he did not initially intervene in the course of things.

The "Lutherans," as the Christians from the Church of the Gospel are soon called and call themselves to Luther's annoyance, are justifiably proud that toward the end of his life the elector openly subscribed to their creed and forsook everything that functioning as the rear guard had seemed to require up to that time. The first German-language service is held on April 9, 1525, in the elector's chapel in Lochau, in the presence of the already deathly ill Frederick. In his hour of death, he receives Holy Communion under both kinds and finally has Luther called to his bedside. But does this mean that Frederick leaves the old Church whose awakening he had wished to hasten? Does he even finally "unreservedly adopt a new creed" as has been said? And does he die alone because Luther cannot hurry to his bedside for the reason that the distance is too great?

Here also, the real consolation of history is an altogether different one. However natural the self-confirmation that Lutheran Christians find here may be, the real consolation lies in the insight that it was precisely during this critical phase that there were leading Christians who, like the elector and his Junker Jörg, remained loyal to the Church. Holy Communion under both kinds certainly was no betrayal of the old Church. Nor did Luther abandon his dying elector. For to console him, he wrote him

that he would die with Christ and in the community of the saints who, through their justice, virtue, and love, would intercede for his sins and his still imperfect love.

From the Wartburg Luther grappled with his adversaries. His harassed friends Spalatin and Melanchthon and some printing presses had their hands full publishing his polemical tracts and treatises such as the one against Hieronymus Emser, "the goat of Leipzig," or against the theologian J. Latomus of Louvain, and on monastic vows. What especially enraged Luther was that, "against his better knowledge and from pure greed," the cardinal archbishop of Mainz had opened an exhibition of his relics in Halle to see if the depressing game of indulgences for money could be played some more. Luther reacted promptly with a cutting tract, *Against the Idol at Halle.* But at the instigation of Wolfgang Capito who, in spite of a clearly reformist persuasion, had entered the service of the archbishop in late 1519, the elector and Spalatin prevented the publication of the pamphlet. Yet Luther saw to it that a vehement written protest was transmitted to Mainz which the cardinal answered immediately with an incomprehensibly humble apology.

After this, not much time passed until it became known that the man who was generally believed to be dead was very much alive indeed. While this does not mean that his hiding place was discovered, the "secret services" which already existed at that time now began their inquiries and thus made Luther's safety increasingly precarious.

IV

1. NEW "REFORMERS" AND "REVOLUTIONARIES" ENDANGER THE REFORM

Luther could consider the letter from Mainz as a kind of success. But from his beloved Wittenberg very disquieting and then alarming news reached the Wartburg.

It all began with the tiresome question of celibacy. Luther was troubled when, in the name of "evangelical freedom," monks and nuns suddenly started deserting their convents. His unease increased when his respected colleague Karlstadt—once again ahead of his time—suddenly became engaged to the young Anna von Mochau and promptly married her on January 19, 1522.

It is not at all remarkable and perfectly in keeping with our modern experience that, at about the same time, the reform of the liturgy which Luther planned to undertake after returning from the Wartburg became an urgent need. Again it was Karlstadt but also the Augustinian Gabriel Zwilling who forged ahead. They composed an "evangelical mass," did away with the abomination of private masses, and polemicized against the veneration of the sacrament outside of mass. Luther had become so restless that, at considerable risk, he traveled secretly to Wittenberg on December 2 to find out first hand what he could about this stormy development. And during the next few days, the first tumults did in fact occur: armed students and burghers drove the priests from their altars, mocked the monks in the Barfüsserkloster, and interfered with their private masses.

The elector who had earlier appointed a commission threatened punishment, but even he could not keep the pot from boiling over. Broad segments of the community backed the demand for "liturgical reform": free preaching of the gospel, the abolition of private masses, the lay chalice, and, to prove a superior morality, the closing of inns and whorehouses.

In spite of another prohibition by the authorities and in order to create a fait accompli before the elector could intervene, Karlstadt again took action: for New Year's Day, he announced the first "German mass"—it was actually celebrated at Christmas—with the words of consecration spoken out loud, without the Canon, ceremonies, and priestly vestments, without confession preceding the mass, and with communion under both kinds. The impression was enormous. At their chapter meeting on January 6, the congregation of German Augustinians left it up to the friars to decide whether to abandon the monastery. Those who remained were to earn their bread as preachers, teachers, or craftsmen. Begging was henceforth prohibited. On January 11, Zwilling gave the signal for the attack on images and side altars which were forcibly taken from the churches. A few days later, Karlstadt, who wished to avoid trouble, arranged for the official removal of the images by the magistrate.

But the pot kept boiling. For suddenly the "Zwickau Prophets," the weavers Nikolaus Storch and Thomas Drechsel, together with Melanchthon's former disciple Markus Stübner, made their appearance in Wittenberg. Their concern is not the reform of the liturgy but the Holy Spirit who guides them directly by the "inner word," whereby they can readily do without the "outer word" and the sacraments but especially—and this has a familiar ring—infant baptism. They are terribly "moral" and "spiritual" and dream of hanging the priests and the godless so as to finally institute "God's Kingdom." Melanchthon, in whose house Stübner finds lodging, is disquieted but impressed by a doctrine that one cannot simply reject.

But because no prompt intervention could be expected from the elector, and because the cathedral chapters, university, and magistrate were helpless in face of what was happening, Melanchthon and the council turned to Luther and requested that he return to Wittenberg. The situation left Luther no choice, the elector seriously warned him not to come back because he could not protect him, but it is likely that he secretly awaited his return.

Luther's prompt decision is typical of his personality and his understanding of reform. It was characteristic of both the man and the Christian that every time he found himself in a life-threatening crisis, he confronted danger with poise, serenity, and total commitment, yet not without skill, reflection, and even reserve.

After his arrival in Wittenberg on March 6, 1522, Luther, for the first time and at the very beginning of the actual Reformation, has to deal with "adversaries" from his own camp. He is guided by concern for the Church and the gospel. Archconservative that he is, and instinctively opposed to all tumult and violent overthrow, he obeys both the will of the elector and the decree of the Imperial Governing Council.

He quite literally breaks the resistance of the citizens and the people by the power of the "word." From the first through the second Sunday of Lent, he spends every day in the pulpit of the parish church, his tonsure newly trimmed and wearing his monk's cowl, and preaches against all those who, without considering the weak, propose to make a new law out of the freedom according to the gospel. Except for private mass, everything the overly zealous reformers had abolished is reinstated. Even the service Luther will elaborate in 1523 will still contain a Latin mass although there is no mention of sacrifice.

The discussion with the originators of the Wittenberg reforms leads to major complications. Karlstadt vigorously resists the abolition of the "order" he has inspired and insults Luther, calling him "a neo-papist." Luther defends himself indirectly at first, then strikes back by openly attacking the "fanatics" (Schwärmer). In this process, slogans are first heard and limits are apparent that become typical of the Reformation.

Luther discovers that his mysterious and painstaking effectiveness as "father in the faith" (he never referred to himself by that term, of course, however fond he may have been of identifying with Abraham and Paul) is matched by the not altogether fortunate impact of his works, which was much more immediate than could ever have been anticipated. By his carefully worked out biblical lectures, his unusually extensive activity as a preacher, his printed sermons, his devout writings and countless, very personal letters, his catechisms and hymns and his translation of the Bible, he became a "father in the faith" to many but this occurred in a process that is very difficult to describe. While at the Wartburg, he translated the New Testament in eleven weeks. The translation of the Old Testament, on which other experts and scholars collaborated, dragged on until 1534. While minor critical objections can be made to it, the Luther Bible, which made countless printers rich and never returned a penny to its author, is not only creative in terms of its language but, more importantly, a spiritual achievement. It is, quite literally, God's powerful and creative Word which comes to man through Luther's mouth and which, by its very nature, cannot remain without effect. No one, whether Protestant or Catholic, should dispute this, however critical one's attitude toward Luther may otherwise be.

But the impact of this work over time is a wholly different matter, for that is something which the author is no longer solely responsible for, nor is he in most cases its direct cause. Nor did it unsettle Luther that other Christians and other "reformers" suddenly appeared and filled out the ecclesiastical space that he had created in their own way.

In November 1521, from the Wartburg, Luther had already demanded the immediate abolition of private mass in a aggressive tract, De abroganda missa privata, but its prompt publication had been prevented by Spalatin. He not only demanded the abolition of this form of the mass and the abuses it gave rise to but he also disputed the notion of the mass as sacrifice in general. Theologically, both points are closely connected. For Luther believed he had understood the following ominous nexus: anyone who, remembering the "once for all" character of Christ's sacrifice on the cross, makes sacrifice anew, so that in return for a small stipend the infinite fruit of the indefinitely repeatable offering of the sacrifice of the mass might benefit certain of the living (to aid them in all that troubles them, from a toothache or syphilis to the urgently implored death of a bothersome fellow human being) or the dead, misuses not only the mass but avails himself of the sacrifice of the mass to justify the abuse. As the title of the German version of the tract, Vom Mißbrauch der Messe ("On the Abuse of the Mass"), clearly indicates, Luther's more virulent criticism does not directly address the sacrifice but merely a false notion of sacrifice as the basis for the entire abortive development. Yet this polemically pointed rejection of what is in fact an untenable view of the mass as sacrifice had a negative effect on Luther's doctrine of the mass. For the inclusion of the Christian in Christ's sacrifice—a fundamental concern that Luther never surrendered—can now no longer be grounded in the original, properly understood sacrifice but occurs through the "Word" and without visible relation to the mass. Despite laudable liturgical reforms designed to make it more of a congregational service, the mass loses importance, because although respect for the sacrament of the altar increases, it becomes no more than communion, to be celebrated after the sermon. But because Luther unswervingly held to the true presence of the Lord under, in, and with the bread and the wine, and to the reintroduction of communion under both kinds, the reduction of the mass to mere remembrance which can be observed in Reformed churches did not take place.

Thus it came about that in the course of the intra-reformist differentiation of creeds, the real presence of the Lord in the sacrament became an article of faith over which, even after Luther's death, people and confessions will differ.

Through his protest, his unyielding demands for corrections, and his intransigence in matters of truth, Luther not only involved himself in states of violent tension with most other reformers—quite apart from his animosity toward "papists" and "fanatics"—he also isolated himself to a considerable degree and allowed himself to be isolated where the development of a new ecclesiasticism or negotiations over ecclesiastical policy at the imperial level were involved. Since negotiations were not his strong suit, he participated only reluctantly and suspiciously in the intra-reformist religious discussions as in Marburg (1529) or at the Wittenberg accord negotiations (1536). He did not join at all in discussion with representatives of the old Church, because an exchange of views with the "Antichrist" simply made no sense to him. Yet his relationship to the hopelessly decadent papal Church was closer, more positive, and more deeply rooted than that with "fanatics" and "sectarians," between whom and reformers such as Karlstadt, Müntzer, or Zwingli he hardly differentiated.

Although his readiness to negotiate was nothing like Melanchthon's and Melanchthon's passionate efforts to prevent the splitting of the Church, Luther remains for the Roman Church the extremely bothersome but irreplaceable partner in a reform which he himself did not bring off but which no one acting without or against him has been able to carry out to this day.

2. LUTHER SHOCKS
THE PEASANTS BY HIS JUDGMENT
AND THE DEVOUT BY HIS MARRIAGE

Nothing makes clearer how alien Luther can seem to us than his position on the Peasant's War which began in the spring of 1524 with the uprising of the Stühlingen peasants in the southern Black Forest and quickly spread into Swabia and Alsace, the Tirol and Carinthia, Franconia, Thuringia, and Saxony. Our contemporaries, attuned as they are to social issues, are especially offended by Luther's role here. Such a perspective makes it impossible to create understanding for Luther's position, and we must content ourselves with defending him against the most serious criticisms and present his concerns in their oddness but without distortion.

We may be certain that neither a questionable nor a political motive prompted Luther to adopt a position which is incomprehensible to many. He did not act as the princes' lackey or servant of established power, and was even less "the mindless, soft-living flesh in Wittenberg," the "father of obsequiousness," "sycophant," and "Doctor Liar" that his former admirer Thomas Müntzer, a man with an equal talent for trading insults and giving tit for tat, accused him of being. In his great "programmatic writings," he had made himself the speaker for a reform which, despite constant warnings against the "carnal" misunderstanding of the gospel, certainly did not exclude man's daily life, nor his longing for liberation from injustice and for the fulfilment of legitimate social desires.

There can be no doubt that Luther's reform contained very important suggestions for this-worldly reform and that therefore the peasants like the knights before them certainly did not lack justification in invoking Luther. Moreover, in his tract *Von weltlicher Obrigkeit, wieweit man ihr Gehorsam schuldig sei* ("How Far Obedience to Secular Authority Must Go," 1523), he not only had resisted interference by the secular powers in the ecclesiastical sphere but had threatened divine wrath in severely criticizing tyranny and the willfulness and unlimited greed of princes in their dealing with peasants and burghers. In the middle of April 1525, the peasants turned directly to Luther. A delegation handed him the twelve articles with their demands. Everybody expected Luther to come down in favor of the peasants. The articles were so moderate, and this not just from today's point of view, that even Duke John who had taken over the business of government from the dying elector would have been willing to accept them. Luther had a "fruitful talk" with the delegation, offered them food and drink, and promised that he would soon take a position. But the answer, *Ermahnung zum Frieden auf die zwölf Artikel der Bauernschaft in Schwaben* ("Admonition to Peace on the Twelve Articles of the Swabian Peasantry"), in which he warns the peasants "not to misuse God's name," the manuscript of which was finished at the end of April 1525, was the start of all the troubles that followed.

Sounding conciliatory, Luther nonetheless warns the peasants against confusing the two realms which would destroy secular authority and prevent the preaching of the gospel. How can the peasants invoke God's name and Christ's example if they go against Scripture by committing violence and refusing to obey authority? Luther reacts with particular annoyance to the demand that "servitude" be abolished "because Christ freed all of us." Anyone who argues like this understands "Christian freedom" carnally, according to him. For as a Christian, a serf certainly enjoys "Christian freedom." But those who wish "to make all equal" turn "Christ's spiritual realm" into a "secular and external one," and also threaten the order of the "secular realm" which is based on the "inequality" of people. Even the experience of injustice does not give the Christian the right to rebel against authority. But Luther also warns the lords emphatically not to abuse their power and admonishes them to stop "oppressing and taxing" the peasants.

In spite of all historical explanations—the serf of the Middle Ages was no slave and in Bavaria, for example, serfdom was not abolished until 1818, and in Russia not until 1863—and in spite of the modern insight that equal rights also create new dependencies and that one can even hang oneself on the "golden rope of freedom," Luther's fundamental thesis here makes excessive demands on our understanding. Even the significant observation that as theological postulates his demands do not preclude "social development" under "secular responsibility" does not make our contemporaries more sympathetic.

But to the disappointment of the peasants and of modern Christians, things go even worse. For before the first tract which had been printed in May was published, Luther had written a second one in which, impressed no doubt by the unimaginable ferocity of the war and especially the atrocities committed by the peasants in Weinsberg, he turned indignantly and with great vehemence *Against the Robbing and Murdering Mobs of Peasants*. Going beyond all permissible bounds, Luther now called on the princes to strike without pity. He takes the peasants for devils, their defeat for a divine service; they are to be slain like mad dogs.

Although the princes hardly needed Luther to encourage them, they carried out the slaughter with frightening savagery. As previously in Swabia, Württemberg, Franconia, and Hesse, Philip of Hesse and the dukes of Saxony and Braunschweig inflicted a crushing defeat on an army of eight thousand peasants near Frankenhausen on May 15, 1525. Thomas Müntzer who, confident of divine protection, had driven the fanaticized peasants into battle escaped into town but was discovered in his hiding place and executed a few days later after having been horribly tortured. All in all, one hundred thousand peasants were cruelly killed: shot, burned, beheaded, or blinded and maimed. The result was ghastly and can be excused neither by a conceivable motive nor the cruelty of medieval war.

In view of the horror of this, and of all later and all future wars, we do not propose to go searching for lame excuses for Luther. But we should realize that such an observation does not advance us any and that Luther's conduct affords no grounds for asserting that he was partly to blame for the awful end result. Although I do not consider speculation useless, I believe that it is idle to wonder whether the revolution of the peasants under Luther's leadership would have brought epochal social change. For the sake of the unpleasant truth, it must be noted that weighty theological reasons made it impossible for Luther to assume responsibility for a revolution. The catastrophe he foresaw for the peasants and which he surely did not want was, he felt, the lesser evil and the ineluctable punishment for their rebellion against God. All he can plead from a human moral point of view is this: his commitment was motivated by no opportunism of any kind. He did not make his decision in order to please the princes but because he considered rebellion unjust. And he made his decision although, along with the majority of his contemporaries, he was convinced that the revolution would be victorious which would have meant his certain death. In view of the situation, he therefore also had to acknowledge that without him the peasants' uprising would never have reached its terrible dimensions. In this sense, Luther assumed his guilt in 1533 when he said in a *Table Talk:* "Preachers are the greatest of all slayers. For they urge the authorities to execute their office strictly and punish the wicked. In the revolt I slew all the peasants; all their blood is on my head. But I pass it on to our Lord God, who commanded me to speak thus."

The talk is unusually harsh and Luther will have to take responsibility for it. But we note that in the tradition of the papal Church, in which the justice of the sword which is unacceptable to us is at home, a saint of the rank and quality of Bernard of Clairvaux said nearly the same thing when, faced with the horrible defeat that ended the crusade, he had to take responsibility for his advocacy of it before the European public.

His position in the Peasants' War is not the last move that provides food for thought in this context. For right in the middle of that situation, this unusual man shocks us with the personal decision to celebrate his wedding with the former Cistercian nun Katharina von Bora, on June 13, 1525. The judgment that Luther gambled his immense prestige and lost is historically correct. The Reformation was no longer a popular movement. The authorities began taking up the cause of Luther and the princes' Reforma-

32 View of Marburg on the Lahn with the landgrave's castle and the church of St. Elisabeth. Mediated by the landgrave Philip of Hesse, the religious colloquy between Luther and Zwingli took place here between October 1 and 3, 1529, but differing views of the Lord's Supper prevented agreement. Whereas Zwingli interpreted Holy Communion as no more than a symbolic remembrance, Luther always upheld the real presence of the Lord in the bread and the wine. After the colloquy made the divergence between the two definitive, the fifteen Articles of Marburg were published. Fourteen of them expressed a common conviction, and it was only on the question of the Lord's Supper that agreement could not be reached.

33 Ulrich (or Huldreich) Zwingli (1484—1531), the reformer of German-speaking Switzerland. Having been a priest at the cathedral in Zurich from 1519, he began to oppose the old Church in 1523 after he was won over to the idea of the Reformation by the reading of Luther's writings. A different conception of the Lord's Supper caused marked opposition to Luther.—Painting.

34 Doctor Martin Luther. Painting by Lucas Cranach the Elder (1528).—Weimar, State Collection in the castle.

HVLDRYCHVS ZVINGLIVS

TRIÆ QVÆRO PER DOGMATA SANCTA SALVTEM;
RATO PATRIÆ CÆSVS AB ENSE CADO

OBIT AÑO DNI, M.D.XXXI, OCDOB XI
ÆTATIS SVÆ XLVIII.   EX

IESVS

Venite ad me omnes qui labo-
ratis et onerati estis et ego
reficiabo vos tollite iugum
meum super vos et discite a
me quia mitis et humilis
sum corde et inve-
nietis requiem
animabus
vestris

35   The gathering of the Evangelical estates at the Diet of Augsburg during which, on June 25, 1530, the Augsburg Confession was solemnly presented and read before the emperor and the empire. Philip Melanchthon had formulated the articles of the Confession because Luther, being an outlaw, could not be present. Luther commented: "I do not know what to improve or change nor would that be appropriate for I cannot step so lightly."

36   Christ as redeemer on the cross. Center section of the altarpiece in the town church of Sts. Peter and Paul in Weimar. The altar, donated by the elector Johann Friedrich who is shown with his wife and son on the inside panels, is the last work of the older Cranach and was completed by his son Lucas the Younger in 1555. The old painter can be seen standing next to John the Baptist and his friend Martin Luther to the right of the crucified Christ. Luther is pointing in the open Bible to the last verse of chapter 4 of the Epistle to the Hebrews: "Let us then with confidence draw near to the throne of grace, that we may receive mercy and find grace to help in time of need."Above, we read: "The blood of Jesus his Son cleanses us from all sin"(1 John 1:7), and on the second page of the Bible the following quotation from John 3:14—15: "And as Moses lifted up the serpent in the wilderness, even so must the Son of man be lifted up, that whoever believes in Him may have eternal life." These three passages aptly interpret the multiform theme of this altar: sin and redemption.

37   View across the old town and toward the citadel of Nuremberg. Here, Emperor Charles V had to conclude the Peace of Nuremberg because of the Turkish threat. Signed in 1532, it granted the members of the Evangelical Schmalkaldic League religious freedom until the council would be convoked.

38   The Katharinenportal on the Luther house in Wittenberg was constructed in 1540 by Katharina von Bora and was a present to her husband. The Luther house was the former "Black Cloister" of which the elector made a free and unencumbered gift to Luther in 1532.

tion began. Instead of a congregational Christianity and the free election of pastors, we see the rise of the territorial and national church from which demanding and alert Christians suffer to this day.

From Luther's perspective, things look quite different. Leaving the Reformation aside for the moment, we will try to arrive at a somewhat better understanding of his late decision to marry.

The perfectly straightforward human point of view seems the most appropriate to begin with. Luther was forty-two and at the height of his powers, as his contemporaries liked to say. While his friends concern themselves about their families and are taken care of by their wives, he sits, alone and deserted, in the tower of the Black Cloister, with much work and many failures, poor as a churchmouse and uncared for like a desert father.

If one wishes to criticize Luther's decision, this sad reality must be taken into account. And when one does one will modify one's critical judgment by first noting that it was not Luther who abandoned the monastery, as the mass of his fellow friars did before him and an entire army of monks and nun did in the sixteenth century; it was rather that the monastery collapsed around him, as it were.

Luther did not reject monasticism after he had allegedly recognized it as a typically "Catholic" miscarriage of life in the faith and because he thought it was irreconcilable with his "reformist discovery." He remained a monk longer than his fellows and would have continued unhesitatingly in a monasticism that fulfils its vow to God by the liberating tie of love and does not see itself as the indispensable path to salvation or raise itself above the rest of Christendom as a "state of perfection." But in an empty monastery, such a life became and still becomes impossible and meaningless in the course of time.

At just this time (and here, as is customary in marriage, accident played its mediating role), there lived in Nimbschen convent near Grimma an apparently high-spirited group of twelve Cistercian nuns, who, lacking Luther's staying power and theological understanding, were affected by his critique of monasticism. The young nuns, who most assuredly had not yet died to the world and who, like the twenty-six-year-old Katharina von Bora, were by no means certain of their calling, had heard of the great Doctor Luther, studied his writings, and quickly found reason why, in their particular case, the omnipotent and fearsome God would mercifully exempt them from fulfilling their vows. After the early death of her mother,

Katharina's father had quickly remarried and simply sent the unwanted daughter into the convent where her aunt Magdalena, for similar reasons, had earlier found a home. These aristocratic ladies, none of them over fifty and one the sister of Vicar General von Staupitz, had written to friends and relatives imploring their help in escaping as quickly as possible. The friends and relatives had then turned to Doctor Luther, and the Doctor, with his feel for real emergencies, had promptly taken the reluctant "brides of Christ" under his wing. For in 1523, when this story really begins, he was not yet the busy man he later became (that he was already thinking of unwashed dishes or the holes in his socks is not very likely, considering his basic talent for monasticism).

Catholics will take delight in the clever and circumspect "Catholic" manner by which Luther, still in his dusty and

Signatures of reformers on the Marburg Articles of 1529: Martinus Lutherus, Justus Jonas, Philippus Melanchthon, Andreas Osiander, Stephanus Agricola, Johannes Brenzius, Johannes Oecolampadius, Huldrychus Zwinglius, Martinus Bucerus, Caspar Hedio.

worn Augustinian cowl, and his Lutherans resolved what was in fact a Catholic problem. Leonhard Koppe from Torgau, councilor and tradesman, a friend of Luther's and purveyor to the convent, took on the mortally dangerous and seemingly blasphemous part of the enterprise when, during the stillness of Easter eve, he kidnapped the virgins, hiding them in empty herring barrels and transporting them in his covered cart through Duke George's territory and on into Torgau in Electoral Saxony. In the light of Easter morning, a short distance this side of Torgau, the valiant Koppe and the jubilant women intone the Latin Easter sequence. On this occasion, one already notes the cultured alto voice of the young Katharina, a woman whose name always appears last on lists but who will soon prove to be "first."

In Torgau the former Augustinian Gabriel Zwilling takes charge. Under his supervision, the ladies of Torgau provide a change of clothing, and we may assume, considering the herring barrels, also a quick bath. But before the "unhaltered heavenly brides" have a chance to delight in typically Catholic joie de vivre and the vanity of fashion, the strict Pastor Zwilling returns and escorts the *rebellantes*, their heads modestly lowered, through the Nonnengasse to the Easter service in St. Marien where, in a mighty sermon, he makes clear to the congregation and the fleeing nuns what the flight from the "false" to the "true" Church means. Then decent Koppe takes over, for he has prepared a feast for the none too frightened ladies, and as they sit down to Easter lamb and abundant Torgau beer, they taste the first pleasures of a new life whose table and holiday manners show no sign of any "reformation."

It is in the final act that we can really let ourselves go in ecumenically liberating laughter or in *risus pascalis* (Easter laughter) at the "dumb devil." It begins as the three-horse carriage with the "honest virgins" arrives in Wittenberg on Easter Tuesday where the entire population is up and about. Koppe, whom Luther celebrates as a "blessed robber," is the hero of the day, while Luther must set about matchmaking since only three of the twelve are taken back by their families. With the remaining nine, he had as many worries as debts, although he did not fear the latter inordinately, considering that he had vowed poverty and that even without the vow poverty would remain his faithful companion throughout his life. The other worries are more serious and not susceptible of a theological solution which Luther, undeterred, proposes to the public in writing in April 1523. But this does not get the virgins married. Luther then writes to Spalatin and any number of people; his friends lend a helping hand; and the ladies secretly do their share, since it is their weddings after all that are at stake. The situation is not altogether clear. Nikolaus von Amsdorf intends the oldest of the nine, his aunt, for Spalatin, but says nothing about other prospects. Yet such prospects certainly existed, especially for the younger nuns. The older ladies of Wittenberg who know life begin thinking more and more about the Doctor. But when the honest virgins appear on the scene, they think of the devil. Thus Luther discovers that as "reformer" he cannot make matches as he wills. His worn cowl suddenly becomes a problem: if he is to continue wearing it, he needs a new one but a new one costs money, and at this moment he needs that for Katharina. He therefore does not have one tailored for himself and there is no one who will make him a present of one. But in his new role, he can no longer wear his dirty habit, although Katharina has nothing to do with that, of course. Where to lodge her for the moment is much less of a problem: he cannot bring her into the Black Cloister, although space there is abundant and the dirty dishes are piling up. But once the idea strikes him, it won't let go. But it is unnecessary to put her up there just now, for she is staying in Master Philip Reichenbach's house and then moves to Lucas Cranach's where there is a good deal of work to be done, with not only the famous studio but a printing shop, a pharmacy, and a busy inn to be seen to. Here Katharina can demonstrate that the role of "Martha" also offers opportunities for making oneself indispensable. No less a person than King Christian of Denmark, who was lodging at the Cranachs' at the time, made Katharina a present of a golden ring, something Martin did not care for and a gesture that makes one wonder. Luther, every inch the reformer, holds back and insists that Hieronymus Baumgarten, the scion of a patrician family in Nuremberg, finally make up his mind to marry the "bride of Christ" who had been intended for him. But in Nuremberg they don't care for run-away nuns and the plan comes to nothing. But no one is sad in Wittenberg: certainly not Katharina, for she had known from the start that she didn't want to go to Nuremberg. Nor does the Doctor mind, for with the passage of time he has grown accustomed to the idea and is tired of thinking in circles all of which lead back to Katharina. Still, nothing is resolved. Then, suddenly, something happens, and event follows event in rapid succession. And the terrible peasants' affair rather than impede developments actually hastens them. This is how Luther is, how he thinks and acts—eruptively and abruptly, as back in Stotternheim. Having hesitated for years, he will not wait one more day. He has a bad conscience neither about leaving the Augustinians nor about the peasants and accepts a situation that not he but God created. He has nothing to hide for he does not "burn"; he loves his Kate and cannot be ashamed of it. Melanchthon is exasperated because he is thinking, and not without good reason, of the hue and cry of the papists and the peasants. But Luther cannot and will not be a hypocrite; the peasants actually lend urgency to the situation: he will marry his Kate "to spite the devil" and before they kill him, just as he still wants "to plant an apple tree before the Day of Judgment," an apocryphal phrase but one that characterizes him well. He knows he will not change the course of history but will not await the return of the Lord alone.

He thus takes the decisive step without any false pathos. On the evening of June 13, 1525, Johann Bugenhagen blesses the engagement in the Black Cloister with the faithful Justus Jonas, pastor of the castle church, Johann Apel, professor of canon law, and Lucas Cranach and his wife as witnesses. In great haste, Luther has a marriage bed made so that the nuptial ceremony can be appropriately carried out. Husband and wife climb into the bed and remain there for a moment hand in hand—Luther very serious, Katharina with a transfigured smile, and Jonas, who reported it all, with tears in his eyes. A few tears go along well with the laughter of this moving moment. For the marriage that is being blessed and witnessed here became one of the happiest in all of Christendom. It lies at the origin of the Protestant parsonage and serves as an example to this very day. As a love blessed by God, it also strengthens the love of those who renounce marriage for the same reason. Luther was as capable of renunciation as he was of married love. We should not worry needlessly why he finally decided in favor of the latter. Nor should we be concerned for Katharina. For in her love of Luther, she made true and fulfilled what she had somewhat hastily promised Christ as a sixteen-year-old girl.

Luther did truly celebrate the feast of his love with his Kate, although certainly not with indifference to the sorrow of that terrible war "when rivers and brooks ran red with the blood of the peasants." It is very likely that Katharina suffered more from these conditions than her unyielding husband. Although from a noble family, she would surely have permitted a little more revolution if only because then her Martin would not have lost his heroic image.

It speaks for the couple's love that Luther did not melt like wax in the arms of his wife and that Kate submitted to her fate, although in all this-worldly matters she soon "wore the pants." This marriage is truly a great mystery: Luther marries, yet in his commitment to others he remains what he always was. And the earthy and receptive Katharina develops the kind of devotion she had promised in Nimbschen but would probably not have attained had she remained in the convent.

V

1. LUTHER AND THE FURTHER DEVELOPMENT OF THE WITTENBERG REFORMATION

Although the marriage does not constitute a break in Luther's spiritual development but rather a climax which had an unusually fruitful effect on his intellectual and theological creativity, it is yet an external and corollary sign of a change in his attitude toward the Reformation which was due to other causes. Here, also, one cannot speak of a break in his position and service in behalf of the Church, for he continued to be the "authority" from which everything of importance emanated. And however one might judge that authority, it had to be reckoned with whether one criticized, modified, or rejected it. Yet typical shifts of the focal points in his life and activities occurred and in back of these lies that change, although personal reasons of course also played a role.

That Luther did not experience this transformation as something negative, as a decline, but rather as an upward movement he owed primarily to his Kate—abstracting, that is, from his unshakable faith and the qualities of his character. For the first time, at the age of forty-two, Luther had something like a private life which extended beyond the intimacy of the couple to the little community of the family which expanded in turn to include the circle of friends, table companions, disciples, and all those in need of such a community. Anyone who has brethren who at an advanced age have dared take the step from monastic or scholarly solitude into marriage knows the difficulties that make such a step a risky venture. In the case of Luther and his wife, there is no trace of problems. True, he must accustom himself to much that is new, for all the life around him cannot cover up the fact that a new and different phase has begun. Luther is about to concentrate on the internal task that confronts him. The advocacy of his reformist concerns in the outside world, vis-à-vis emperor and empire, the papal Church, the "fanatics," and other reformist churches, indeed the constitutional elaboration of the Church and its guidance by the Wittenberg reformation—all this he increasingly shares with or even leaves to others. This was a normal development which Luther himself initiated, welcomed, and permitted. (Despite his genius and originality, he never rejected "team-

work.") Yet both to Luther and those whose activities now bring them into the foreground, the change mentioned above is clearly perceptible in all of this.

This is true even of a task Luther never surrendered: the mostly polemical discussions with his adversaries and the fight to keep his original concerns pure. Whether Luther attacks Karlstadt, Zwingli, Bucer, or the pope and the papists, his criticism is no longer accepted uncritically in all cases. This is true even of the noticeably decreasing number of cases where all believe that Luther has to move into the front lines because everything is being threatened and only he can answer persuasively. This can be impressively documented by the great dispute with Erasmus which finally came in spite of the fact that those most directly involved did not really want it.

Erasmus was already at work when, in the spring of 1524, Luther politely but firmly advised him once again not to attack his teaching. The *Diatribe de libero arbitrio* ("Diatribe on Free Will") had been published in the fall. In it, Erasmus finally took a position with the calm, competence, and superiority which he owed to his reputation and addressed himself, as Luther conceded, to the central question.

After some hesitation initially, Luther answers Erasmus, without noisy polemics but with unusual decisiveness, in *De servo arbitrio* ("On the Bound Will"). This tract belongs to the few works that Luther characterized as his best and we must take this estimate into account. But there is no overlooking the fact that to this very day, scholarly judgment is not unanimous. This applies equally to Erasmus' position. The controversial treatment of this extremely difficult problem cannot be set forth here in detail, and the problem itself certainly cannot be resolved.

In all disputes between fundamentally different points of view, one deals with fundamentally different presuppositions which are tantamount to prejudgments. If one decides for Luther's point of view as one studies the introduction—and that is my position—one has already decided against Erasmus.

The controversy with Erasmus marks a turn in Luther's life although it cannot be further defined. Having grasped that, one will not misunderstand certain other aspects of that life, such as the fact, for example, that he suddenly spent so much time with his family, that (probably thinking of Frederick the Wise) he tried to fill Kate's stocking by working a lathe, and that when this attempt failed because he had not skill for it, he sometimes busied himself in his garden where he successfully and not without pride planted small apple trees, grew and harvested vegetables, and nonetheless espoused the right of birds because they, like the rest of suffering creation, were waiting for God finally and definitively to make man better with his "precious Last Day." Luther did not withdraw into private life and, more importantly, did not degenerate into a Sunday gardener, however. Apart from his enormous activity as preacher and lecturer, he devoted himself with much intensity to the further reform of the service and the teaching of the Church. In 1526, he continued the necessary reform of the liturgy with *The German Mass,* the *Pamphlet on Baptism,* new hymns, and the transformation of the old choral into perfectly singable German church music. In 1529, he created the *Large* and the *Small Catechism for Ordinary Pastors and Preachers* through which he has remained the catechist for Evangelical-Lutheran Christianity to this day.

In another sphere which really fell under the purview of the bishop, Luther remained the competent "authority" although, strictly speaking, Johann Bugenhagen as the pastor of Wittenberg should have fulfilled this task. For on May 14, 1525, during the congregational service, Luther ordained Georg Rörer who had been called to assume the office of the Wittenberg archdeaconate. This was his first ordination and it took place without the pomp of the old ritual though not without the laying on of hands. It will be shown below that Luther did not understand this act as "evangelical investiture or introduction," as generations of Lutheran theologians thought, but as ordination according to the example and the precepts of the Apostles. As early as 1523, in response to an inquiry from the Bohemians, he had studied the question how one should install suitable Christians in Church office when papal bishops refused ordination and there was only the dubious possibility of having candidates ordained by subterfuge which meant that willing Italian bishops assumed this task in exchange for large sums of money. For many Christians but especially for many theologians of both creeds, Luther's answer was not what one might expect ("You are all priests; simply choose a pastor and install him"). Rather, he explained himself somewhat cumbersomely but with remarkable clarity: "If the Church as a creation of the Word needs the Word to live, and if the Word falls silent without the office, then you have the

right and the power of emergency ordination, just as you have it in the case of baptism which is necessary for salvation." Thinking of the future, Luther acted with this in mind in the case of deacon Rörer, although the hordes of ordained priests and monks who had gone over to the Reformation amply sufficed to fill all pastoral needs, and the Wittenbergians, especially Melanchthon but Luther as well, had not yet given up the hope that the connection with the old episcopate could be preserved or reestablished.

This brings us to another task which was primarily assumed by the princes acting as "emergency bishops" and the ecclesiastical or secular visitors they appointed, the hiring of pastors according to canonical law not yet being far advanced. I am referring here to pastorates and parishes in the various districts which had already been neglected during Catholic times and which, under the conditions of the transition, naturally took on a special urgency. While Luther's involvement in this matter was only indirect and advisory, an important field of activity opened up for Melanchthon, Spalatin, Myconius, and other tested churchmen. Melanchthon wrote his *Instructions to the Visitors* which Luther revised and supplied with a preface and which first appeared in 1528.

The year of the plague, 1528, saw the publication of the *Confession Concerning Christ's Supper* in which Luther summarizes and attests to his faith. Although he was aware that as a single Christian he could not speak in the name of the Church, he did not hesitate to say that he wished to commit posterity to his confession. This personal confession is the overture to the elaboration of the creed by the Wittenbergians in which Luther played an active part as the Articles of Schwabach and Marburg show. But another work which he was writing concurrently is as important and revealing. This is the *Von der Wiedertaufe an zwei Pfarrherrn* ("Letter to Two Pastors on Rebaptism") in which he not only expounds his positions on rebaptism and the Anabaptists but also on the "Church of the Antichrist." However horrible its situation may be, the Church, even as Church of the Antichrist, remains the "true Church." Even more, the Antichrist proves it to be the Church of Christ, for he will not appear among the horde of sectarians. Everything Luther has comes from the "Church of the Antichrist."

The phrase "the elaboration of the creed" summarizes a process which, more than any other, makes visible the change that Luther undergoes. History provides the overture: although Clement VII had not forgotten the "Sack of Rome," his defeat at the hands of Charles V in 1527, he bowed to the inevitable. Since he had no weapons left with which to fight Charles V, he, like his predecessors before him, used the consecrated oil of investiture and coronation—not the "stinking chrism," as Luther liked to call it (centuries earlier, the original chrism had been replaced by the oil of catechumens)—whose particular charism it was to make one's political adversary the effective "protector of the Church" and the "patrimony of Peter." After this had been accomplished in Bologna, the emperor recalled the religious question he had neglected in Germany and which, in connection with the newly arising Turkish threat, had attained a new virulence. What no one had dared hope any longer could be read in the emperor's proclamation by which, even before the coronation, he summoned the princes and estates of the empire to the Diet of Augsburg on April 8, 1530. In addition to measures to deal with the Turkish danger, the Diet was at long last to attempt to heal the split in the faith and the Christian religion, renouncing all dispute and doing justice to both sides, so that "as they are and fight under one Christ, so they should also live under one Church and in unity."

In Germany, especially in Electoral Saxony, people had faith in the proclamation because they wanted to have faith in it. On the elector's order, the Wittenberg theologians worked out a draft for the Augsburg negotiations. Luther participated as an advisor but the so-called Articles of Torgau had been written by Melanchthon. The draft was both very simple and very optimistic: the reform of ecclesiastical usages will be defended before the emperor and empire, which is the reason the working paper is initially called *Apologia*, considering that in this sphere especially "many abuses" had caused strife. Should a justification of doctrine become necessary, one would fall back on the Articles of Schwabach. Luther had certain reservations about this conception but nothing is known of a veto against it.

Luther also obeyed the elector's order to accompany him at least as far as Coburg. The hesitation that is apparent here had clear legal and political motivations: being an outlaw, Luther could not simply present himself at the Diet. From the very beginning, it was clear that he would be excluded from the actual negotiations although he was wanted in an advisory capacity. Talks between the elector and Nuremberg led nowhere and Luther therefore could not accompany the delegation beyond Coburg castle.

On Sunday, April 3, 1530, Luther leaves Wittenberg with Melanchthon and Jonas and meets Spalatin and the elector's party in Torgau. In Saalfeld, Johann Agricola and Kaspar Aquila who are escorting the count of Mansfeld join the party which arrives in Coburg on April 15. While Luther preaches in the town church on the suffering and cross of Christ, the elector orders Melanchthon to work on the introduction to the *Apologia*. When it is determined that Luther may not even go as far as Nuremberg, he takes up residence, accompanied by Veit Dietrich, at Coburg castle in the early morning of Pentecost while the delegation sets out for Augsburg after the morning meal.

It appears that Luther thought very little or, more honestly, nothing at all of the negotiations in which the elector had placed considerable hopes and Melanchthon all of his. Although no one said so publicly—and this is still the case today—mistrust was mutual. The "leading intellects" of the Augsburg delegation, not including the excessively trusting Jonas and the faithful Spalatin, mistrusted Luther because they knew their own plans. Besides, it was so very easy to keep the "jewel of the Reformation" safe from harm in his Coburg solitude: no one could see Luther without electoral permission. Luther's secretary, Veit Dietrich, who was devoted to the reformer reported to Melanchthon who should have known how Luther was and what "devils" he was fighting at the moment. This perfect system had a single flaw which could not be completely eliminated: it was not really possible to forbid Luther all writing and his printers all printing so that, not being fully employed as advisor nor wholly content with that role, Luther soon had the somewhat outlandish notion to "admonish" the ecclesiastics assembled in Augsburg from his mountain in his own wilful way. Once again, Luther found himself in "Junker Jörg's" situation but no longer had the freedom of movement he had enjoyed at the Wartburg. But such is life in the Church: things inevitably become "public property," the author an "advisor" in negotiations about an important issue which has long since ceased being his. Melanchthon will have a similar experience with the Augsburg Confession: although he works on this important document during the following weeks only as an editor, he will deal with it at the Diet and during the next few years as if he were its author until his work becomes a creed and is expropriated so that he no longer has any say over its meaning.

Within certain limits, Luther's task as "advisor" was probably seriously intended and actually feasible. The question was whether he was really meant to participate in

39 Martin Luther. Life-size portrait of the reformer by Lucas Cranach the Younger. 1575. Collection in Coburg Castle.

40 View of Schmalkalden. Here the Protestant princes and towns created the Schmalkaldic League to defend themselves against attacks on the Reformation by Charles V (1530). In 1535, the life of the league was extended by ten years. In 1536/37, Luther wrote the Articles of Schmalkalden which were intended as the basis for negotiations for a council to be held in Mantua. They are considered Luther's theological testament. While the defeat of the troops of the League in the battle at Mühlberg in 1547 put an end to the League, the emperor failed in his fight against the Reformation because the resistance of the German princes was too great.

41 In 1518, Philip Melanchthon (1497—1560) became professor in Wittenberg and Luther's leading collaborator. With his *Loci Communes* (1521/22), he created the first Evangelical dogmatics, and with his *Instructions for Visitors* the basis for the internal structure of Lutheran churches and the training of Evangelical clergy. Melanchthon formulated the Augsburg Confession and had a share in the elaboration of the Articles of Schmalkalden and the various religious colloquies, as with Zwingli in Marburg.—Painting (1543) by Lucas Cranach the Elder, Florence, Uffizi Gallery.

42 Interior of the castle church in Torgau which was the first Evangelical church to be built and was consecrated by Luther on October 5, 1544. In his inaugural sermon, Luther defined the task of Evangelical churches: "that our good Lord may talk with us through His sacred Word, and that we in turn talk to Him through our prayers and songs of praise."

43   John Calvin (1509—1564) became a reformer in 1533. But in his *Institutes of the Christian Religion* (1536) which was accepted in Geneva as the constitution of both church and state, he deviated from Lutheran teaching. The Reformed Church as founded by Calvin became the driving force of world-wide Protestantism (Huguenots in France, Calvinists in the Netherlands, Puritans in England).—Painting (16th cent.) in Geneva, Bibliothèque publique et universitaire.

44   Johannes Bugenhagen (1485—1558) belonged to Luther's inner circle and was his confessor. In 1523, he became town pastor in Wittenberg and professor at the University. His activity as reformer had the geographically most extensive and organizationally most enduring impact, for he created the Evangelical church and school order for Pomerania, Braunschweig, Hamburg, and Lübeck among others. On February 22, 1546, he gave the funeral oration for Luther.—Detail of a baptism of Christ donated by Bugenhagen, by Lucas Cranach the Younger in the town church in Wittenberg.

45   Luther died on February 18, 1546, in Eisleben where he was born. The painter Lukas Furttenagel of Halle drew the reformer's face, marked by age and illness, as he lay on his deathbed. Berlin, Kupferstichkabinett.

46   Luther's grave under the pulpit of the Wittenberg castle church.

the negotiations and whether he would feel that he truly was a participant. For to merely play the role at the "Diet of the daws" that had been picked for him in Augsburg was impossible for Luther even if the elector tried to run the show himself.

At first, everything went well. As yet, there was nothing to "advise" since Master Philip had first to find his bearings in Augsburg where the situation looked quite different from what one had imagined at Torgau. None other than Johann Eck must be blamed for this since he proposed once more to help truth prevail. In four hundred articles, he intended to show and refute before emperor and empire all the heresies Luther and his followers had committed. This meant that Melanchthon had to introduce the already prepared *Apologia* of the reforms with a summary of the most important doctrinal teachings. Work progressed rapidly, yet he had bad dreams: an evil spirit transformed him, the high-flying eagle, into an ordinary tomcat and put him into a bag to drown him. Luther did not forget this vision: toward the end of August, heedless of all dangers, he wanted to rush to Augsburg to free the "eagle" from his prison. What he could not know, was not meant to know, and never discovered was that Philip had found himself in the "bag" much earlier, although the end of August was the second time he got caught.

From the very start, Luther could not have been satisfied with what he heard. Only this explains the fact that he never became active as advisor. For when, on May 11, the elector sent him the quickly written document so that he might examine and revise it thoroughly, and Melanchthon wrote him with great urgency on the same day and for the same reason, he sent a brief answer of five lines on May 15: he liked the document as far as it went and felt that corrections or additions were neither necessary nor fitting since he could not step as lightly as Master Philip.

Although he tried very hard, Melanchthon could not wheedle him into making further statements on this the principal subject of the Diet. On May 20, he asked him again and then, annoyed, stopped, and remained silent until June 13. This in turn annoyed the mistrustful Luther. After a strong warning, he angrily accepted "Junker Schweigler's" declaration of war and stopped writing letters as of June 7. He did not even open the imploring letters written with tears which Philip sent him after June 13 and especially during the critical phase of the document's public reading. The famous *Confessio Augustana*, or Augsburg Confession, thus came into being without Luther's participation if not without his laconic assent. Not until

two days after the solemn reading, on June 25, did a hailstorm descend on Melanchthon and the other friends from Coburg castle. One must read these splendid but terrible letters (misleadingly called *Trostbriefe*, "consolatory letters," by Luther scholars because they were requested to console the trembling Melanchthon) if one wishes to understand the profound difference between Luther and Melanchthon and his humanistically inclined friends.

However good the intention, however understandable such an effort on the part of the churches of the Reformation may have been, the crack that Luther's letters created could not be plastered over on this occasion. Even more, this crack would have widened into a definitive break, with consequences that are difficult to gauge, had Luther known of the political solitaire Melanchthon was playing, initially developed in conversations with the archbishop of Mainz in June and embarked on, immediately after the emperor's arrival, with the help of the Spanish secretary of state Juan Valdes, a confidant of Cardinal Gattinara who had died on the way to Augsburg. This sentence is enormously long because it tells a very sad story which occasionally surfaces in the scholarly literature but is then repressed or obscured again because it stains the memory of the "Augsburg confessor." The project that Master Philip tried to realize with Spanish help between June 15 and 21 was overwhelmingly simple: the Protestant princes and estates would renounce the solemn reading of their creed. In exchange, they would make known their demands reduced to the lay chalice, the marriage of priests, and the mass in German, and the emperor and the cardinal legate Lorenzo Campeggio would see to the restoration of the unity of the Church.

This grandiosely simple plan came to nothing because the elector, represented by Chancellor Brück, did not give Melanchthon the requisite consent on June 21. But none of the princes criticized Melanchthon's independent initiative, nor did anyone object to Luther's being kept in ignorance of the entire matter. Melanchthon and his enlarged group of co-workers now had to finish the neglected Augsburg Confession without further delay. The task was barely completed before the solemn reading on June 25 in which the disappointed Melanchthon did not participate. In spite of everything, the valiant princes thus became the "confessors" of the true faith after all, and even Luther praised them for it.

On July 4, Melanchthon began the second round of negotiations with Cardinal Campeggio, who allegedly loved him "like his own son" and also had a high regard for the still celibate Brenz (celibate although the widow he was going to marry was already waiting for the wedding in Schwäbisch-Hall). For why should it be impossible to accomplish with the Confession what admittedly could have been more easily achieved without it?

The tenor of the famous letter which Melanchthon wrote to Campeggio in this matter (and which, having been circulated everywhere except at Coburg castle, caused unease even in Venice) was, from Melanchthon's point of view, fully justified by the Augsburg Confession as he understood it. (We must not blame the author for the missive's devout curial style.) The unreserved acknowledgment of the authority of the Roman Pontiff or the readiness of the Roman Church to content itself with a tacit, totally non-binding tolerance of Protestant demands, both of them elements that went beyond the Confession, will simply be toned down by later statements, or forgotten. But to the considerable disappointment of Melanchthon and his friends, and in spite of this extreme obligingness, the second attempt will also fail.

Luther, who sensed something but never heard about the decisive event, became increasingly impatient among his "daws": "Go home, go home, you confessors. I will canonize you if you finally break off these pointless negotiations." But when his own people publicly accused Melanchthon of having let himself be bribed with Roman funds, he stood like an angry bear in front of poor Philip.

In a paradoxical but ultimately credible way, Luther finally took a position on the Augsburg Confession: on the one hand, he straightforwardly faulted it for "stepping too lightly," but on the other, he celebrated it as the great, fundamental, and unifying confession. His first verdict shows that he never opposed it as such but simply objected to the aims and methods of negotiations that attempted not only to attain the impossible, that is, *concordia in dogmatibus* as distinct from an achievable "political peace," but which, in addition, jeopardized truth itself in that they proposed to reconcile "Belial and Christ," "Luther and the pope."

It can be seen that "negotiations" between Luther and the cardinal were an a priori impossibility. For negotiations (today we somewhat prematurely and globally call them "dialogue") make sense only where the two sides encounter each other as willing partners. But neither the cardinal nor the pope were willing and so the entire plan finally failed. Still Campeggio pretended to be ready to negotiate for some time, and Melanchthon made it all too easy for him to adopt that stance. Furthermore, one can

exclude the notion that Philip would have proposed these concessions and the cardinal have accepted them had they simply contravened the gospel. For wouldn't the lay chalice and a married clergy have been a legitimate concession for preserving the unity of the Church? And wouldn't the recognition of the German mass have provided the opportunity of giving to a simple eucharistic celebration the full meaning of the Lord's Supper, which the Roman side had lost sight of?

Here lies the abiding rightness of the plan and also the reason why Melanchthon tried, with anxious singlemindedness but certainly innocent of any treacherous intent, to realize it without and even against Luther.

But it must also be noted that this "relative right" of Melanchthon's procedure can be justified neither factually nor objectively. Still less does it suffice to put Luther and his unyieldingness in the wrong. Quite the contrary is the case. From Luther Philip should have learned—and all of us can learn—how, in spite of all singlemindedness and passionate willingness to reach an understanding, a negotiation does not deteriorate into a "horse trade" which, at the expense of truth, creates a unity that ultimately we have as little capacity to create as we do the justice through which we are justified before God. He could have learned from Luther how even seriously conducted negotiations can remain a genuine "dialogue" during which we do not simply talk at, and listen to, each other, but where, more importantly, the one is heard who alone speaks the liberating and unifying word of truth.

If one follows Luther, one may negotiate like Melanchthon, for one will be immune to the temptation of a "homemade ecumenicity" which, because it makes the concessions expediency demands, destroys the very thing it seeks to bring about. Ecumenicity does not end but begins where, as in the demanding dialogue with Luther, we allow ourselves, on the basis of a shared faith, to be led into that "unity" which is never a matter of our choice.

2. THE FINAL YEARS AND ULTIMATE THINGS: "COME SOON, LORD JESUS!"

On October 13, 1530, Luther finally returned to his Kate and the children, his book and his Black Cloister. He had mourned his father, fought the devils in the air, emptied many a flask of wine, and prayed even more. Despite constant headaches—"my head is like a cathedral chapter"—

he had worked like a man possessed. His hope was unbroken; he was in the midst of a new project, but knew more about the "change" and the conditions of the end-time which casts doubt on all our plans. Only one thing still counted, and that was that we "keep still" in our faith and await the "precious Last Day" with joy.

Because nothing of earthshaking importance will occur, we may call the fifteen years Luther still has left to live with his family and for Christianity the final ones, a period of literally ultimate things although penultimate ones occurred, of course, and life in the Black Cloister went on.

In June 1531, Luther's mother followed his father. She had been privileged to witness the Doctor's life and activity in Wittenberg and to sing her grandchildren to sleep. Now, the son consoles the dying mother with the words of Christ: "Be of good cheer; I have overcome the world." And he also writes: "Everyone, my children and my Kate, are praying for you. Some are crying, some eat and say, grandmother is very ill. May God's grace be with us!"

During these final years, he spends more time teaching and training students. In 1531, he lectured once more on Galatians, his favorite epistle, his "Katharina von Bora," as he also called it. From 1535 to 1545, he lectured again on Genesis, the "histories of the fathers," and especially the story of Abraham which runs through his entire work like a red thread. In numerous important disputations in which he proved again that one can be both biblical theologian and scholastic, he tried to head off his fundamental concerns from developing misunderstandings. And he preached now and then as he always had and served piety through numerous writings.

Not necessarily among the "ultimate things" is the *Table Talk*—in which Luther comments on the events of the past, present, and future before friends, colleagues, students, and members of his household and which, as occasional speeches, deal now humorously, now angrily, sometimes crudely, not always correctly but usually relevantly and pointedly with topics from all spheres of life and knowledge. Written down and supplemented by eager students—V. Dietrich, C. Cordatus, A. Lauterbach, G. Rörer, and J. Schlaginhaufen are some of the "stenographers"—entire collections came into being which naturally have a special interest for publishers and whose significance for Luther's biography would be even greater were "truth" and "legend," the "authentic" and the "merely decorative" more easily distinguishable.

Painful for Luther at this time were the deviations from the core of his doctrine of the law and the gospel that close and even very close friends were guilty of. There was the ever renewed dispute with Johannes Agricola who repeatedly quarreled, first with Luther and then with Melanchthon, because he disputed the permanent meaning of the law, holding that its demands were excessive as compared to the gospel. In spite of a close personal friendship which also included the two families, an unfortunate dispute arose which, with its polemics against the recalcitrant "Master Grickel," finally led to Agricola's expulsion from Wittenberg. Melanchthon, conversely, arrived at a doctrine that seemed to maintain—as Conrad Cordatus reported to Luther immediately after the lecture—that "good works" had to be considered a "necessary condition" of salvation. Luther was deeply disturbed that such a split in fundamental beliefs occurred even during his lifetime, and among his closest collaborators at that. In this case also, a quarrel developed and the peace-loving Master Philip suggested to his friends that he would not be sad to see the ties holding him in Wittenberg finally break, for he would prefer devoting the rest of his life to scholarship.

Resisting misunderstandings and making essential decisions about the future, Luther had to return to the question of church office. For after the failure of the Augsburg negotiations, it had to be accepted that "Catholic bishops" would not ordain pastors for Protestant congregations. At the same time, there was a marked decrease in the number of priests from the old Church aligning themselves with the Reformation. But everywhere, in cities like Augsburg and in the countryside as well, voices invoking the priesthood of all believers could now be heard that laid claim to the right of emergency baptism and emergency confession for all laymen, and also to the "freedom" of the head of household to administer communion to his family. Luther resolutely rejected all these demands and soon did so with considerable vigor. In 1535, he created the first German ordination formulary according to which, once the examination had been concluded and a congregation had called them, the ordinands were ordained centrally, in Wittenberg. To justify ordination by the Wittenberg pastor, Luther invoked the example of Augustine who had first been "consecrated or ordained to preach" by his bishop Valerius and had "become a bishop himself" after Valerius' death and then went on to ordain a great number of "pastors or bishops" in his "pastorate." It is consistent with this that Luther later created an ordination rite for bishops, ordaining Nikolaus von Amsdorf bishop of Naumburg in 1542, and Prince Georg von Anhalt coadjutor bishop of Merseburg. Since both ordinands had already been ordained and Luther rejected "re-ordination" throughout his life, we may infer that, in practice, Luther did not object to the old-church distinction between presbyteral and episcopal ordination. Although Luther protested strongly against the claim to power on the part of the bishops of his time, his criticism fell silent whenever bishops made the pastoral office of Christ visible and effective through their ministry. Bestowed *ritu apostolico* and sanctioned *voce apostolica*, the bishop's office was therefore hardly a human invention as far as Luther was concerned, however testily he may have reacted in all those cases where pope and bishop put forward the mandate of the Lord ("Feed my sheep," John 21: 16 ff.) as their "divine right."

Luther's remarks regarding the impending council were of similar importance. It is not enough to point to the unquestionable ambivalence of the statements. For years, people had referred to this council because they felt it was their only salvation. Since they knew or thought they knew that the papacy would never assent to a council because it feared for its power, invocation of it gradually came to resemble a political veto that cost nothing but also produced no results. When news finally did become more definite and the possibility more likely, reactions were cautious and skeptical. One was aware of the dangers a council called and directed by the pope would have for one's own cause. Yet to refuse to attend was not a possible alternative. During the first phase, there was thus a good deal of jockeying as during the odd meeting between Luther and the papal legate Vergerio on November 6, 1535, in Wittenberg.

The situation became much more serious when Paul III finally did announce that the council would open on May 13, 1537, in Mantua. Now, the evangelical side had to take a position willy-nilly. In addition to the possibilities mentioned above, the elector considered a counter-council of Protestant estates and theologians.

Because the problem was considerably more weighty than in Augsburg, the elector did not turn to Melanchthon but asked his chancellor to call on Luther himself. He was to determine which articles absolutely must be defended before the council and where room to maneuver without danger to one's conscience existed. The draft Luther was asked to prepare would be examined by other evangelical theologians and then given its final form. Luther completed his Articles of Schmalkalden in January

1537. They are clear, consistent, and uncompromising: there are, first, the doctrinal articles in which nothing can be yielded. And with a view to its character as a sacrifice and the abuses connected with this, the mass is rejected with uncommon severity whereas existing common elements go unmentioned.

The position on monasteries and the veneration of saints is more positive. Luther's rejection of the papacy is uncompromising, but he observes accurately that recognizing the papacy as an institution of "human law" would be of no service whatever to the papists. Yet this was precisely the concession Melanchthon was prepared to make as he attested in a special reservation he added to his signature.

The elector Johann Friedrich enthusiastically backed Luther's articles and wished to have them accepted at the meeting of the Schmalkaldic league in Schmalkalden on February 10. On February 7, the elector, accompanied by Luther, Melanchthon, Bugenhagen, and Spalatin arrives in Schmalkalden. While Luther assumes the duties of pastor as usual, Melanchthon joins up with Philip of Hesse and the Strassburgers and sabotages the acceptance of Luther's articles in order to avoid doctrinal disputes over the Eucharist among the Protestants. Compared with his position in Augsburg, this meant a one-hundred-and-eighty-degree change in Melanchthon's "coalition" and position. He thus prevented acceptance of Luther's articles as the "official confession" for years. But being the editor of the Augsburg Confession, he was now asked to supplement it by a tract *On the Primacy and the Power of the Pope.*

Luther, who had not attended the official negotiations because he was ill and suffering from kidney stones had become so sick in the meantime that one feared the worst. His face in tears, Melanchthon prays at the bedside of his hopelessly ill friend. This time, also, there is no reason to doubt the sincerity of these tears, yet the scene illustrates the mystery of a friendship which cannot really be illuminated when one makes the distinction between person and issue.

As though by a miracle, Luther recovered. Dislodged by the shaking of the carriage which is to bring the dying man back home to his Kate, the stones pass through the ureter and Luther feels newborn. As when he was kidnapped to the Wartburg, people again believe he has died. At the urging of the princes, he must certify from Wittenberg by his signature and seal that his death is a favor he unfortunately cannot yet do the devil, the pope, and his enemies. God, he writes, had not wanted him yet, but the day would come when He would, although at that moment his enemies might wish that he were still among them.

Luther is clearly perfectly well again and everything he always was whenever he appears in public: drawing back like a hammer-thrower, he fights for and against everything that threatens him during these final years: *Against Usury, Against the Turk* (1541), *Against Hans Worst* (1541), *Against the Roman Papacy, an Institution of the Devil* (1545). Oddly enough, he no longer has any trouble with electoral censorship during these years. True, even now, the reformers do not proceed in a completely coordinated manner. Once again, it is Melanchthon who drafts for his Wittenberg colleagues a proposal for a "gentle Reformation" (1545), and Luther signs although he is already strenuously at work on his "testament" against the "Antichrist" on the Roman throne, the illustrations for which are being provided by Cranach's woodcuts ridiculing the pope, with a terse commentary in verse.

In connection with this eschatological theme belongs a final topic for which Luther has been publicly denounced and will unquestionably be denounced again in this jubilee year. I am thinking of the "Jewish question" regarding which our ever so peaceful public, anxious to make amends for the past, seems inclined to paint Luther and ultimately all his concerns in blood-red, as if he were the man without whom Hitler and his horrible final solution for the Jews would never have come about. Since the gentlemen who want to write history with the "paintbrush" understand little of real history, historical pointers won't do much good in this context. To mention, for example, that the exemplarily peaceful Erasmus wished even ghastlier things on the Jews — a fact that, oddly enough, no one cares to call attention to—cannot exculpate Luther. The same is true of predecessors such as St. Bernard and his contemporaries. It does not help Luther and does not explain a great deal when other highly respected names are painted on the walls of houses below or above his.

I therefore content myself with the statement that it is very unjust to denounce Luther in this matter. I am also aware of the fact that the very summary proof which I will offer here will convince neither the public nor the people with the brush. But in the case of all those who do not consider themselves infallible, the following remarks should at least initiate a revision of the customary misjudgment.

1. Luther's anti-Semitism had nothing whatever to do with any kind of racial theory. On the contrary, throughout his work, Luther rejects and combats any national theology that identifies the seed of Abraham with God's people.

2. Luther's position on the Jewish question cannot simply be inferred from his five works that deal with Jews but only from the place they have in his theology as a whole. From that perspective, the uncompromising harshness of the late writing on the Jews is neither a symptom of senility nor the expression of a hate neurosis but the result of the growing eschatological seriousness of the situation. Neither the murder of God for which the Jews are blamed, nor the crimes they are charged with, and certainly not the avarice for which they are forever criticized (and which bad Christians use as an excuse for not paying their debts), but only the "eschatological" intensification of the situation accounts for the uncompromising harshness. The Church can accept the fact that Jews will not convert. But what it cannot accept is Jewish missionary activity and the infiltration of the Church by the Sabbatarians. The fight against Jewry and its doctrines therefore necessarily becomes something like the fight against the "Turk" or the "Antichrist" though an effective defense against the latter does not exist.

3. But most decisive is the fact that, from his early to his late work, Luther never modified his theological interpretation of the "murder of God" which is normally the principal motive for Christian anti-Semitism and all persecution of the Jews. The Jews crucified Christ as representatives of Christianity and all humankind, yet God saves us by transforming the death of His son into the cause of our salvation. The same idea is expressed in a new verse of the Wittenberg songbook of 1544: "Our great sin and grievous misdeed have crucified Jesus, the true Son of God. But for that reason we cannot call you, poor Judas, and the rest of the Jews enemies, for the guilt is ours." Although this verse has not been explicitly ascribed to Luther, there are a number of statements that justify such an ascription (H. H. Oberman).

This brings me to a concluding thought which should fit in well with this willful and meandering biography, yet causes me considerable difficulties for a variety of reasons. Instructive conclusions would be inappropriate and superfluous: the reader does not need our assistance to infer them from our portrayal. But a long farewell that would attest to my love for Luther as "father in the faith" could easily be misinterpreted as sentimentality and hagiography. I will therefore dispense with edifying conclusions, and especially with a detailed account of the truly Christian death that finally overtook him in the early morning hours of February 18, 1546, in Eisleben, where he had presumably come into this world sixty-three years earlier. His last words come from the Latin Compline of his monasticism: *In manus tuas commendo spiritum meum, redimisti me, Deus veritatis!* ("Into your hands, I commend my spirit. You have redeemed me, God of truth".) And later a scrap of paper is found bearing this message in his handwriting: "The truth is, we are beggars."

I wish to take leave of the living Luther by presenting two snapshots that strike me as typical of his life in the face of death.

The first shows him on his last birthday in the bosom of family and friends, on November 10, 1545. He had wanted a final celebration with the kind of joie de vivre that is never irreconcilable with the thought of death. The elector had recently restocked the wine cellar, and in the kitchen of the Black Cloister Kate is busy preparing a hundred pounds of pike and sixty carp. The tables are buckling under the weight of steaming dishes. The jug of golden Rhine wine or perhaps Franken wine is making the rounds, and the mood is the same as one would find at an unending banquet of a king. Two generations of reformers have come to celebrate: his friends Melanchthon and Bugenhagen have been given the best places, while Cruciger and Major sit further away. There is much talk until, as usual, the Doctor rises to give one of those great speeches whose conception will forever be a mystery—wild like a charging elephant that tramples everything in its path, yet also tender as an elephant's trunk which can pick a fragile butterfly from blooming roses without causing a single leaf to fall to the ground. Toward the end, there is an intimation of death and Luther speaks of it, roughly and unsentimentally, so that Kate will have reason to scold and need not weep, yet full of expectation and longing: "When I return from Eisleben, I'll lie down in my coffin and give the worms a fat doctor for their dinner. I am weary of the world and so depart all the more willingly, like a guest from a common inn."

The second snapshot comes from the "Great" Genesis commentary, the final lecture of which he gave November 17, 1545, and more specifically the preface which Luther had used as an introduction to the first volume of his works which, supervised by Veit Dietrich, had appeared in print a year earlier.

The unusual preface was written under the impression the reading of the Abraham story, which he loved more than anything, had made on Luther. Abraham died as a stranger in his own country but he died as the friend of God. Even during his pilgrimage, he lacked for nothing, not even the four hundred shekels of silver he needed to buy the cave of Machpelah near Mamre from Ephron the Hittite so that he might bury his Sarah there. When, years later, he died at a very advanced age and "tired of life," his

Luther's handwritten entry in the Bible printed by Lufft in 1541:

Ps. 41

In the book I have written,
My God, I gladly do thy will.
Through this doing gladly, or obedience to Christ,
we are all sanctified (Hebrews 10). As St. Paul
says in Romans 5: Through one man's obedience many
are justified. Such things will one study in this book.
Thus it will be understood.

Mart LutheR D.
Anno 1542

sons bury him at the same place. The prologue begins with a short statement on the purpose of the lecture: from the very beginning, it had not been meant for publication. Rather, he gave it to serve the Wittenberg school, his audience, and himself in order to practice the preaching of God's word and to avoid sitting about lazily in an otherwise useless old age. He thanks the *collectores*—K. Cruciger, G. Rörer, and V. Dietrich—for the trouble they took in going through the manuscript (what a pity the original text of the lecture has not come down to us) and also regrets the effort that was expended on the improvement of his work. He cannot assert that he commented on Genesis; at most, he had intended to. Although this may be the usual "humble rhetoric" of all prefaces, the following explanation is literally true: "Everything is said *extemporaliter* and in very popular fashion, in my own natural diction, German and Latin intermingled, and much more wordy than I had intended."

But there is no need for big words. For it is Scripture, "the Scripture of the Holy Spirit" which he has tried to interpret. And who can do this after the Apostles? Then he quotes St. Gregory the Great on the Bible and expresses what he was privileged to discover throughout his life: "Scripture is like a huge stream along whose banks lambs scamper and in whose deep middle elephants bathe." With a view toward all who have interpreted Genesis before him, he says: Not he who has understood everything and made no mistake is the "best," but he who allows himself to be carried away by the "greatest love." In that sense, not even the "fathers" wrote the perfect commentary. "And how downright ridiculous are the modern exegetes who believe they are accomplishing great things when they paraphrase the subject matter of Scripture *pura latinitate* ("in perfect Latin") although they lack all intelligence and understanding and have as much talent for interpretation as donkeys for playing the lyre."

St. Jerome (whom Luther did not really respect) was therefore right when he said that everyone contributes what he can to the construction of "God's tent": "Some bring gold, silver, and precious stones, others only animal skins and goat hair, for the Lord needs everything for His 'tent.'" Luther permitted the publication of his lecture although—and here he is thinking of Christmas—he can offer the Lord no more than "the wretched hair of his goats." But then, looking forward to Christmas inadvertently turns into the eschatological longing for the return of the Lord who will perfect the work He has begun within us and will hasten the great day of our redemption which we await with heads held high and with a "pure faith" and with a "good conscience"—even though love may be in need of perfection.

Thinking of Abraham and of Christmas, of his own death and the "precious Last Day," Luther ends with the final verses of the Book of Revelation: "'Come soon, Lord Jesus!' (as the Spirit and the Bride prompt one another). And let everyone who loves you say, 'Come soon, Lord Jesus! Amen.'" How silly that expression was that for centuries we believed hit the nail on the head: "To lead a good life one must be Lutheran; to die a good death, Catholic." Anyone who follows Luther will live well and die even better, for at the end of the dark tunnel stands someone who loves us and to whom we can look forward. That is Luther's ecumenical legacy for which we should give him thanks.